Mathew Carey

Pamphleteer for Freedom

Mathew Carey

Pamphleteer for Freedom

By
Jane F. Hindman

Illustrated by W. N. Wilson

HILLSIDE EDUCATION

Cover and interior book design by Mary Jo Loboda

Cover image drawn by Sean Fitzpatrick
based on the cover of the first edition.

ISBN: 978-1-955402-02-6

Hillside Education
475 Bidwell Hill Road
Lake Ariel, PA 18436
www.hillsideeducation.com

CONTENTS

1

A DUBLIN LAD

MATHEW CAREY and his mother stood by the casement window watching for the neighborhood boys to come into view. Faint sounds of voices rising above the moaning of the wind heralded their approach. The murmur strengthened into shouts as a sudden blast of wind swept boys around the corner. Then, Redmond's Hill, a short bit of a street, came alive with shrieking, shoving youngsters. Would it be better for Mathew this time? Mrs. Carey wondered.

As the first of the group appeared, she looked down at her trembling son. "See, Mathew," she said, "they're the same boys your brothers know and play with. Hurry now, or you'll miss them."

Stooping, she pulled the bright blue cap over the ears of the frail nine-year-old and tightened the woolen shawl around his shoulders.

Dread in his dark solemn eyes, the little fellow tried not

to think of the horde of boys about to descend on him as he stared into the fitful Dublin sunshine that blustery March afternoon in the year 1769. Instead, he concentrated on a group of clouds marshaled by great gusts of wind into a vast army charging the sun, then breaking up to re-form into giant squalls. He wished the noisy battalion of children could be dispersed by the gale. But no, the hubbub filled the street and no longer could he ignore the sound of lusty voices.

His mother placed her hand on Mathew's shoulder and gently propelled him away from the window. "Hurry now, here they come," she urged.

Reluctantly, but without a word of protest, the child limped beside his mother to the door, and, leaving the security of her protecting arm, plodded down the steps and across the street to meet the children. As he stepped onto the green, the youngsters swirled around him in a hilarious game of tag. Before he even could draw a breath, he was caught, and boys, like giant tops, spun in and around just out of reach, no matter where he lunged.

"Limpy, oh, Limpy, catch us if you can," they taunted.

As he staggered distractedly first one way and then another, the boys rolled on the ground, overcome with laughter. In a moment, Mathew's big brother John, appearing out of nowhere, clouted a few of the tormentors, then ran to Mathew crying, "Tag me," and without a pause, chased after the fleeing boys.

Mathew, left standing forlorn and alone, looked longingly after his brother, then with head bowed, turned and plodded home.

As he reached the steps, he saw his mother standing in the doorway. Slowly, with his hand on the cold iron railing, he climbed to meet her. Burying his head in the folds of her skirt, he broke into sobs.

His mother's gentle face became grim as she swept her son into the hall and closed the door with a decisive bang. Sighing, she undid the shawl she had so securely fastened a moment before, and sitting on a bench, gathered her son in her arms. She held him close and crooned softly:

"Cry it out, my child. My gossoon is too young to know such sorrow." Tears filled her dark eyes, so like her son's. "Even an Irish lad is entitled to a few years of laughter," she continued fiercely. "God knows we all taste bitterness soon enough, and thanks to others, you have more than your share."

For a long time, Mrs. Carey held her boy, soothing him, trying to make up in love for his sorrow at being different.

When Mathew was born in 1760, his father boasted of the new baby, a bright, whole, and healthy dark-haired boy. For eighteen months he was the happiest of the Carey babies. Then a flighty, new nurse, in a hurry to meet her young man, had let him slip from her grasp and drop on the flagstone floor of the scullery.

"The saints preserve us," she cried, "it's destroyed I'll be, if the missus ever finds out!" Snatching up the wailing child, scolding all the time, she hurried him off to bed.

For a week or so, the nurse kept Mathew away from his mother, who was ill. When Mrs. Carey was well enough to pick up the child, she noticed that he whimpered when she touched his foot. The doctor, when summoned, said that the child's foot had been injured, and asked if he had been dropped.

Mrs. Carey looked questioningly at the nurse whose guilty

blush betrayed her. She was dismissed on the spot, but it was too late to correct the damage. So all his life Mathew Carey was to walk with a limp.

As he grew, the little fellow found it such an effort to drag himself around, that instead of joining the children at their games, he sat in a corner and watched. Both his parents thought he was not very bright, yet hoped that he would be happier if he mingled with other children. But day after day, when he had been sent out to play, after a few minutes, he was always found sitting on the front steps, waiting until his brothers returned from their sport.

After Mrs. Carey had seen the humiliation of her sensitive little boy and listened to his sobs, she never again forced him to go out to be taunted by other boys. He spent his

days listening to the tales spun by his father's coachman, marveling at the stories told by the cook, or sitting quietly in a corner drinking in all that was said by his mother's callers.

Since he spent much of his time with older people, Mathew soon heard of the Penal Laws. He did not know that some fifty years before his birth the English had imposed laws on Irish Catholics that were intended to grind all loyal souls into dire poverty. He did know, however, that they must be bad, for in speaking of them, everyone spat words out as though they made a foul taste in the mouth. Talk, whether in the drawing room or the scullery, was centered about ways of getting around the Penal Laws, but the boy was not exactly sure what they were about until one day when he was standing by his father's knee, admiring his big watch. Looking up, he asked casually:

"Father, when will you be made Mayor of Dublin?"

"Never, my lad, they won't have me," replied his father, offering him the watch to hold.

Mathew's eyes widened. Losing interest in the timepiece, he wanted to know why the best and most important man in all Ireland couldn't be Lord Mayor.

Tucking his watch into his pocket, Mr. Carey smiled at the boy.

"I'm sure they'd not be proud to have a baker as their Mayor, and you're forgetting I'm a Catholic to boot."

"What difference does that make, Father?"

Mr. Carey's face became grave. "Don't you know . . . ?" Rubbing his chin thoughtfully, he continued: "On second thought, how could you know that because of their religion, four-fifths of the inhabitants of Ireland, your father among them, are denied their rights as citizens, being forbidden to vote or hold office."

As Mathew grew older, the Penal Laws were brought home to him, one by one. His next experience was early one morning before the birds had begun to twitter. Wakeful, the lad heard moving about and went to investigate. Voices came from his mother's sitting room; they sounded as though Latin were being spoken, the way their pastor, Father Betagh, did in church.

The boy stole down the hall to the front room and peered through the door that had been left ajar. To his astonishment, he saw his mother, father, the cook, and maid kneeling before a table on which was spread his mother's best linen cloth, with two candles burning on either side of a crucifix. Standing before the table and raising a tiny chalice was the Mr. Hannigan who had come the previous evening for dinner and to spend the night. To add to the mystery, his brother Tom was ringing a small bell just as he did when serving Mass at St. Michael's Church. Glancing up and discovering Mathew at the door, his mother motioned him to come kneel at her side.

After Mass, Mrs. Carey took her son's hand and led him to the priest. "Father Hannigan," she said, "it is time that Mathew shares the burden of the Irish. Will you please tell him what he should know?"

The tall, muscular man, who could have been a sea captain, sat in a big chair and drew the boy to his knee. Taking the frail hands into his gnarled ones, he said solemnly:

"Mathew, my lad, you now hold my life in your hands." He cupped the child's fingers as though he were holding something precious.

The boy looked at his clenched fist, and then into the eyes of the big man.

"You see, Mathew," Mr. Hannigan continued, "I am a priest. That makes me an outlaw. Should you ever tell anyone about what you saw today, I would be hunted and killed and your parents would suffer."

In answer to the lad's questions, Father Hannigan explained that Father Betagh was one of the few priests who were permitted to keep a church open in Ireland and to say Mass.

"But I am one of the hunted priests," added Father Hannigan, holding the child a little closer. "I do not fear that any Irishman will inform on me. My greatest danger is from idle boasting."

"Father," said Mathew earnestly, "you can trust me. Never a word will I breathe. I'll not be an informer."

"That I know well, my lad," answered the priest, giving the boy his blessing. He then rose, saying it was time for him to leave.

After that, Mathew found a corner where he could sit quietly and dream about the priest being hounded from place to place . . . and he, Mathew, frail and though only a lad, protecting him by silence.

From that time on, when the hunted priests and bishops called at the Carey home, Mathew was permitted to listen to their adventures. He compared the lives of these men with the dull existence of Father Betagh who each Sunday said Mass and preached to the same congregation. There was little excitement in this weekly routine.

Every Sunday as they were driving to church behind their old horse, Nellie, Mathew's father would say, "If it were not for the Penal Laws forbidding a Catholic to own a better horse, I'd put poor Nellie to pasture."

But on Monday of Holy Week there had been an accident. Nellie was killed and the carriage damaged. The next day, Mr. Carey drove home in a new carriage behind a fine bay horse. In answer to his wife's question, he said, "This mare was purchased by my Protestant friend, Mr. Quinn, and I have papers to prove it."

Then he added that he had made a handsome gift of money to Mr. Quinn in acknowledgment of his kindness.

When the Careys drew up to St. Michael's on Easter Sunday, the men standing outside walked over to examine the rig. They laughingly questioned Mr. Carey, but he smiled and said nothing.

The church bells drowned out further conversation, and Mr. Carey reached up to lift Mathew from his perch. With his sons clustered around him, he walked down the aisle to the Carey pew where Mrs. Carey and Margaret were already saying their prayers.

Mathew thought the church very beautiful that day. Spring sunshine came slanting through the stained glass windows, casting rainbow hues over the Easter flowers, the colors seeming to echo the Alleluias of the choir.

When it was time for the sermon, Father Betagh mounted the pulpit, removed his glasses, and leaned forward as he always did when he had something important to announce. The congregation listened intently when he told them that the Government had seen fit to abate the Penal Laws enough to permit him to establish a school for boys in Saul's Court off Fishamble Street.

"If any parents care to enroll their sons," he said, "I will consult with them after Mass."

Mathew saw his parents exchange glances. Directly after

Mass, Mr. Carey took his family into the sacristy to speak to Father Thomas Betagh. They found the priest carefully folding the Mass vestments. As soon as he finished, he went to the table, and sitting down, he took up his quill pen and asked how many of the boys Mr. Carey wished to enroll.

Looking down the line of five boys standing beside their mother, he added, "All of them, I hope." Then he amended, "William is too young, I suppose, and Mathew—well, we'll have to decide about Mathew, but I think maybe tutoring would be better for him."

Finally, it was decided that Mathew would go each day to Father Betagh for an hour's instruction after the other boys were finished. So eager was the lad to learn that he arrived at his tutor's long before the appointed time. While waiting for Father Betagh, he sat on a little stool in the failing light and stared into the empty hearth. He fell to wishing the priest would bustle in and throw a turf in the grate to produce a little warmth. In the chill, fears and dreads began to crowd around him. By the time the priest arrived, Mathew had worked himself into a state of terror of his old friend.

From that day on, no matter how he tried, the lad could not throw off the fright he felt each time he entered that room. As a result, he did badly in his lessons.

One winter day, after a year and a half of unsuccessful sessions, his tutor threw his book down in despair. Mathew, in his misery, had kept his eyes fixed on a crack in the wall and failed to answer the questions put to him. Father Betagh was furious.

"Mathew," he complained, "you haven't heard a word I've said all afternoon. Get your hat; I'm going home with you."

The tutor and the pupil walked toward Redmond's Hill in

silence. Half an hour later, Mrs. Carey looked up from the tea table to see the two standing in the doorway. Before she could rise, Father Betagh propelled Mathew into the room, saying, "Madam, I've brought Mathew home. I can do nothing more for him."

"But, Father," protested Mrs. Carey, "he reads all the time."

"Yes, reads what he likes. The lad is fond of grammar, but he closes his mind to aught else," said Father Betagh, shaking his head sadly. "I think your husband is wasting his money. The boy will do as well at home. Good day, Madam."

Although Mathew regretted disappointing his family, he secretly rejoiced in the freedom to read as he pleased. The boy felt a growing desire to learn. One day he came across a French word which he could not understand and had to ask his brother John to translate for him. Humiliated at his ignorance, the boy decided that if his brother could learn a foreign language, so could he. Borrowing a French book, he began to study grammar and memorize a large vocabulary. For seven weeks he burned out his candle each night, scarcely taking time for meals, but at the end of that time he spoke French.

But Mr. Carey, concerned about Mathew's future, felt the boy could not continue in such a haphazard way. The other boys seemed to be planning their own lives, but Mathew was just drifting.

One evening he looked over the top of his paper and said casually to his wife, "Mathew will be fifteen in a few months."

Mrs. Carey, intent on an intricate crochet stitch, replied, "I know, dear, he is growing up."

"Do you know if he has any plans for his future?" her husband asked.

Carefully folding her work, Mrs. Carey remarked that she

didn't know what they could expect from the boy. His foot pained him when he stood too long, and he was so dreadfully shy he scarcely spoke to anyone.

Dropping his paper, Mr. Carey leaned forward, saying, "He'll have to be apprenticed to some trade. I've been inquiring among my friends. If he had been born fifty years ago, I could not have found a master for him. But now—"

When a pained expression appeared on his wife's face, Mr. Carey softened immediately. "Forgive me, my dear, but the boy is in truth fortunate. These days, with the English looking the other way, and with the help of friends, I can get him apprenticed to any of twenty-five different trades—and with good masters, too. It's not every Irish boy that has such a choice."

A week later, Mr. Carey strode into the room as the candles were being lit and the curtains drawn. Mathew, book in hand, stood up to greet his father and help him out of his greatcoat. Mr. Carey went to the fire to warm his hands, remarking that the November night was raw. Then, turning to stand before the blaze, he smiled at the boy, saying, "I've been calling on several of my friends in your behalf, Mathew."

Mrs. Carey paused, taper in hand, to glance at her son.

A shade too casually, Mathew asked, "About my future, Father?"

"Yes, son." His father's tone was kindly. "You know that I have some influence here in Dublin. Many of my friends will gladly take you as their apprentice. Have you any choice of trade that you would like to learn?"

"I have, Father." Mathew threw back his shoulders and stood facing his father quietly, but with an unmistakable air of defiance. His brown eyes were solemn as he set his round jaw and pulled himself to his full five feet six.

"Good, that will simplify matters," said his father. "What is your choice?"

"I intend to be a printer and bookseller," the boy answered firmly.

Reaching forward, his father took the book from Mathew's hand and sent it spinning across the room. "I might have known!" he thundered. "I will not encourage idleness."

Mathew's mother placed a hand on her husband's arm. Affectionately covering her hand with his, he continued in a more reasonable tone: "My boy, you know the Penal Laws as well as I do. You know that the trade of printing and bookselling is forbidden to a Catholic."

"Nevertheless, that is what I intend to be, Father," said Mathew quietly.

"Come now, son, I know you're not fit for some hard trades, but there are many you could learn. Your lameness would be no handicap. How about learning to be a silversmith?"

"No, Father, a printer."

"A wine merchant?"

"A printer."

Father and son stood facing one another. As his father mentioned a trade, Mathew answered with his choice until it became a kind of litany. Before Mr. Carey finished, he had mentioned in all twenty-five trades, all of which Mathew refused, persisting in his desire to be a printer.

Finally his father said, "Where are you going to find a bookseller who will accept you as an apprentice? I will not lift a hand to help you."

"I'll find one," said Mathew confidently.

"Try, my boy, if you wish, but either be apprenticed to a bookseller by the first of the year, or I will see that you are indentured in some trade that I think is wise for you," said his father, then he strode from the room.

"Mathew, Mathew, why do you cross your father so?" murmured his mother, an anxious frown wrinkling her brow.

"It's the only thing I want to do, don't you see, Mother?" Looking down at her troubled face, he said, "No, I suppose you don't. I'm sorry to be such a worry to you, but—" Despairing of explaining himself, he picked up his book and followed his father from the room.

2

APPRENTICESHIP

THE NEXT MORNING, Mathew, his hair in a queue and his shoe buckles polished, set out to find a printer-bookseller who would accept him as an apprentice. Since the two trades were always linked together, the boy did not have to choose between them. Eagerly and with confidence he walked past Dublin Castle and crossed the River Liffey by the Essex Bridge, pausing in its center to gaze down on the city. The day was bright. Sunlight slanted off the unfurling sails of a ship ready to drop down river. Clippers and packets from many nations were tied up at the quays below the Custom House. After watching the ships for a moment, Mathew crossed to the upper side of the bridge to glance at the important business houses huddled together on the north bank of the Liffey. *In which of these would he spend the next few years?* he wondered.

To cover his nervousness, Mathew whistled a jig as he left the bridge and walked up the road. He stopped for a long moment before a sign that read MᴄCᴜʟʟᴏᴜɢʜ—ᴘʀɪɴᴛᴇʀ ᴀɴᴅ ʙᴏᴏᴋsᴇʟʟᴇʀ, then with a forced smile, he entered the shop to speak to the owner.

When the man found the boy wanted to be apprenticed, he said, "No," and turned away.

Even though he had been refused, Mathew found it easier to call on the next man, who looked at him kindly, but stated that he already had his quota and a waiting list. A third prospective employer asked about recommendations, and since there were none, turned the boy away.

Although each of the well-known printer-booksellers found some reason for not accepting him, Mathew refused to give up hope. Since he had spoken to so many different men, he found he was no longer afraid to approach people. But by now he had covered almost the length of the city, and he began to wonder if there were any other printing shops in which to apply. How could he go home and tell his father he would accept another trade?

He was very tired and limped painfully, yet he refused to consider giving in.

By noon, the boy had worked his way down the Liffey to The Bridge. If there were any other printers, he did not know of them. A passerby told him of several more in the slum section called the Liberties.

Never had he wandered through the lanes of that old section, though he had heard many tales of crimes committed there. Desperately anxious to find an employer, he crossed the bridge and plunged into the teeming life of the Liberties.

If he were not so worried, Mathew would have been bewildered and a little uneasy as he walked through dirty streets and cluttered alleys. He was so deep in thought, however, that later he did not remember that he had scrambled out of the path of a child chasing a pig, and never knew that he narrowly had escaped refuse thrown out a door.

A curious old woman who was sitting out in the sunshine, noting Mathew's fine clothes, asked him what he was doing in the Liberties. He inquired about printers, and she pointed out a narrow lane on which a man named McDonnell had a printing shop. He approached a tall, heavy-set man in an ink-spotted apron who lounged in a doorway halfway down the lane.

Mathew stopped before the man and asked, "Please, sir, can you tell me where I'll find Mr. McDonnell?"

"I'm McDonnell. What do you want?" replied the man, scratching his stubbly chin with a dirt-encrusted finger.

"I'd like to be apprenticed to you," Mathew announced solemnly.

The man gave a hard laugh and asked what he would do with another apprentice and a lame one, at that! He already had one lazy boy who did nothing to earn his keep, and besides was eating him into the poorhouse.

Mathew listened politely as the man railed against all apprentices, then he said, "Thank you anyway, sir," and turned away. The few other printers in the Liberties were now his only hope.

The printer reached out and placed a delaying hand on the boy's shoulder, then spun him around. "Hold on a minute," he said. "Don't be in such an infernal hurry."

This lad, who obviously did not come from the Liberties, had aroused the man's curiosity. No one in this section owned a clean ruffled shirt, or fine shoes with buckles. It was a miracle that no one had stolen them.

"How does it happen that your father does not make arrangements to have you apprenticed?" he asked. "You're a bit young for this business."

"My father doesn't want me to be a printer," said Mathew.

"You've run away!" the man exclaimed, as he tightened his grip.

Mathew stood proudly before his accuser and replied, "No, sir, that I have not. I have no call to do that."

McDonnell released the lad and surveyed him from head to toe. "Any father who did not approve of the trade would not pay the apprentice fee," he said, then added that he was a poor man who could not take anyone on without payment.

"My father will pay, sir," said Mathew eagerly. He thought he saw signs that McDonnell was weakening. "If I find someone to take me, he will pay the usual thirty guineas fee."

Thirty guineas! That was more than two apprentices paid in the Liberties. McDonnell's eyes gleamed, but he continued to bargain. He folded his arms and leaned back against the doorjamb, then remarked that Mathew being lame would be slower than other apprentices and that should be worth something extra. When the boy hesitated, McDonnell said:

"Tell you what, my lad, I'll take you, if your father will board you on Sundays and pay for your washing. It's on Sundays you apprentices eat up more than you're worth."

Mathew thought the arrangement reasonable and promised to bring his father to sign the papers on the following Thursday. Then the man, suddenly weary of bargaining, turned into the shop and closed the door. Mathew stood in the alley and looked jubilantly at the place that was to be his lodging for several years.

He had succeeded. He was apprenticed, and to a printer, too! Mathew felt like doing a jig right there in the dirty alley.

If he were able, he would have run all the way home to tell his good news. Instead, he patiently threaded his way through the streets back of St. Patrick's Cathedral, and after several wrong turns, reached the road that led to Redmond's Hill.

That evening, when told the location of the print shop, Mr. Carey raised his eyebrows, but said nothing. He did, however, ask Mathew what the printer had said when he found the boy was a Catholic.

"He never asked me," said Mathew, recalling for the first time that religion was not mentioned.

His father remarked that McDonnell had intentionally not inquired, and agreed to go with his son to make arrangements for his apprenticeship.

That Thursday when they turned into McDonnell's alley, Mr. Carey looked at the run-down building that housed the print shop, then poked his cane in the debris littering the alley, and said seriously: "Think well, son! When I bind you to this man, this will be your home for several years. Can you bear the dirt and squalor?" He waved his stick at a pig that rooted a few feet away. "It is grief you are asking for, that I am sure. My conscience bothers me for letting you do this."

Mathew put a hand on his father's arm and spoke firmly: "Father, I won't do anything else. My mind is made up."

"Very well, my boy," said his father with a sigh. "Let's get this business over."

He opened the door of the shop, and they entered its dim interior which was as poverty-stricken as the exterior. Books, paper, and ink jars were scattered in great disorder. McDonnell came out of the maze to meet them. It took only a few minutes to sign the papers, then father and son were once more on the street.

"Mathew," said his father, "although I disapprove of your choice, I do admire your determination, and hope it carries you through a difficult apprenticeship."

Deaf to his father's warnings, the boy went home to dream of the day when he could begin his new life. He thought the time never would roll around, but at last the year 1775 dawned. On the second day of January, Mathew was up early stuffing into his already overfull box the books he wanted to take with him. Before he had finished, his mother came to tell him that the carriage was waiting to take him to McDonnell's.

At last, having said good-by to all of his family, he was up beside the coachman, his box behind him, driving into the Liberties. He was so excited that he paid no attention to the curses and threats made by men and women as the horse's hoofs splashed them. As the coachman turned into the lane, children swarmed all over the carriage. The coachman flicked at them with his whip, but they merely jeered as they scooted out of his reach. Mathew held the reins while the coachman shouldered the box and dumped it inside the shop, hastening back to the restless animal.

"If you don't mind, Mr. Mathew," he said, I've got to get her out of here before she hurts someone."

Mathew scrambled from his high seat and stood in the middle of the lane to watch the coachman drive off. As he limped toward the shop, he heard a voice behind him say in a high mincing tone, "It's coming up in the world we are. McDonnell will put on airs now he has a dandy for an apprentice." Mathew looked around and saw the speaker lift the tail of his greatcoat between his thumb and forefinger; then holding the coat high, the man danced around the puddles while his audience broke into jeering laughter. Mathew stood in the doorway and joined in the fun. He was still enjoying the joke when a heavy hand fell upon his shoulder, and he looked up to see the scowl of his master.

"Encouraging those scoundrels to make sport of me, eh?" he said. "A fine beginning, I must say." Distressed, Mathew explained that he meant no harm.

"Your kind never do," growled the man, "but there's no need to pass the time of day with the likes of you."

He reached for his greatcoat and struggled into it while he bellowed, "McMahon, come here!"

In answer to the call, an unkempt lad, a year or two older than Mathew, came from the rear of the shop. His shoulder-length black hair, cut unevenly, hung about his ink-smudged face, deepening the blue of his eyes. He smiled uncertainly at Mathew, and the new apprentice's face lit up in response.

"Give Carey a hand with his box and show him where to stow it," ordered McDonnell. "I'm going out."

Without another glance at either apprentice, he flew out the door and down the lane, his greatcoat flapping at his heels. His neighbors, who a moment before had been making fun of him, parted to let him pass, then forgot their game and once more fell into silent idleness.

"Don't bother about him," said McMahon, seeing Mathew gape after the figure. "He's heading for the pub. Won't be back 'til it closes. My name's Tom.

Mathew grasped the half-extended hand of his fellow apprentice and said, "I'm Mathew," adding in a puzzled tone, "Who takes care of the business while he's gone?"

"We do," Tom said. He closed the door, then added, "Don't worry about that. There isn't much business to speak of. Let's stow your box, then I'll show you about."

They hoisted the chest between them and staggered up the ladder to the loft. "This way," said Tom, as he backed toward the window through which a streak of sunshine filtered, casting weird shadows on the untidy stacks of books piled on the floor. Mathew sneezed as they disturbed the thick film of grime that covered the room.

"You'll learn not to kick up the dust," said Tom. "Here is our palace."

Mathew saw a small cleared space in the jungle of books and papers. On the floor was a straw-filled mattress covered by a few rags of blankets. A cracked mug, a small box, and a candle stood on a cloth alongside Tom's sleeping place. The boy hauled a second mattress from on top of a pile of books and placed it beside his own. Mathew poked the pallet so unlike his feather bed at home and remarked that it didn't look very comfortable.

"It's not too bad," Tom replied. "We're fortunate to be sleeping up here. It's warm and dry. At least the Poddle can't reach us up here."

"The Poddle?" asked Mathew, as he stooped to look for his blanket.

"Don't tell me you've never heard of the Poddle?" said Tom as he peered into Mathew's box.

"No," said Mathew, then shook out his nightshirt and looked for a place to hang it. "What's the Poddle?"

"She's the underground river, a cousin to the Liffey . . . But what's that?" Tom asked as he pointed to the garment.

"A nightshirt," said Mathew.

Tom dismissed it with a wave of his hand. He told Mathew to put it away. They always slept in their clothes. Suppose there was a fire and he was caught in such an outlandish thing? They'd be the laughingstock of the Liberties.

Obediently, Mathew stuffed the offending garment back in the box, and returned to the subject of the Poddle. "Where does it surface?"

"The Lord only knows," Tom explained, sitting back on his heels. "She keeps underground until there's a freshet, then she wells up wherever she chooses and gets herself cursed worse than the Penal Laws."

"Is that what causes the puddles in the lane?" Mathew asked.

"It's sitting on top of her this very minute we are, I do believe," answered Tom. "When she bubbles up, we take off our clogs and go wading. It's great fun."

On Tom's advice, Mathew packed his good clothes and put on an old shirt and a pair of dark wool breeches, then slipped his feet into sturdy clogs. Tom gave him a stained leather apron, and, except for his clean face, he was transformed into a duplicate of his fellow apprentice.

"Come, let's go down and look at the shop," said Tom.

They clambered down the ladder to peer among the presses. McDonnell owned very little equipment. He had a large press that was worked by means of a long handle. While Mathew looked on in awe, Tom inserted a sheet of paper and swung the handle to bring down the press.

"Try it, Mat, but don't let McDonnell see you doing it," said Tom, as he showed Mathew the correct position. "We're not allowed to touch the press unless he's here, then you'll swing on that handle like a monkey, until you think you'll die."

Mathew printed his first sheet and thought it great fun.

"Not much it ain't," commented his guide.

Mathew's tour of inspection was interrupted by a small

boy who poked his head through the door at the rear of the shop and called, "Da, Tom, dinner's ready. Ma said to let you know." His message delivered, the child disappeared.

Tom wiped his hands on his apron and said, "Come, Mat. If we don't get to the kitchen right away, McDonnell's little vultures will have gobbled up everything, and there won't be a bite left for us."

He led the way to the kitchen where Mrs. McDonnell, a slatternly woman, was ladling out soup into bowls. Children, squalling and quarreling, swarmed all over the sparsely furnished room. Three were already seated at the trestle table, eating furiously. Mrs. McDonnell indicated vacant stools and filled the apprentices' bowls, then remarked that she supposed that Mathew was the new boy.

"Where's McDonnell? At the pub again?" she asked without much interest.

"Yes," answered Tom shortly, his mouth being full.

Before the apprentices had finished eating, McDonnell arrived, hungry and irritated. A hush fell over the room and all ate in silence, except for McDonnell's remarks on the amount of food they all consumed.

The days that followed differed only in the amount of time McDonnell spent in the shop. Under Tom's direction, Mathew cleaned presses, hauled paper, and distributed type. Tom explained that each little letter had to be distributed or put back into its proper box after the printing had been finished.

The first time that McDonnell stepped out, Mathew examined the books on the shelves. What a poor lot they were, not an interesting title among them. He had no further desire to read them. It was more fun to listen to Tom's fascinating tales about the Liberties. Very soon, Mathew learned to keep out of the way of the master, who chose to ignore him. His fellow apprentice, however, was teacher, friend, and entertainer rolled into one. Tom, in his turn, took on the responsibility of the new boy and protected him from the toughs of the neighborhood.

Saturday night, when it was time for Mathew to go home, Tom insisted on walking with him to the other side of St. Patrick's Cathedral.

"There'll be roistering and brawling, and you not knowing how to care for yourself," he said.

When Mathew remarked that he'd have to learn, Tom insisted, "Not that way, you don't. I'll walk with you."

Mathew was glad for his friend's company, even though in one short week he had begun to look as grubby as his fellow apprentice and no longer could be considered a stranger in the slums. It was unlikely that anyone would bother him now.

As he and Tom walked toward Redmond's Hill, Mathew began to feel very hungry, for McDonnell had said to his wife at supper that Carey wouldn't need any potatoes that night. A bit of bread and tea would hold him until he got to his fancy home where his mother would have a grand meal for him. No need to take food from their mouths, expensive as it was. So, Mathew on his walk home, felt hollow, though in truth, not all week had he left the table satisfied.

When he left Tom and turned into Redmond's Hill, he saw the children as they peered from behind the curtain of his home. They disappeared from the window, then the door was flung open, and the little boys ran out to meet him. He hugged them affectionately, then looked up to see his parents in the doorway.

His mother quickly shooed the younger children off to bed and ushered Mathew into the dining room where candles lighted a well-filled table.

As the three sat down, Mrs. Carey watched her son closely. "Your father thought you would be hungry before bed," she said.

The boy gave his father a grateful smile, then piled a plate high with fish and potatoes, bread and cheese while his mother plied him with questions.

"There's another apprentice, Tom McMahon," he said between bites. "He's about my age, and we get on famously."

Mr. Carey, noting that the lad's appetite had increased enormously, asked, "And McDonnell, what about him?"

Mathew brushed off the question with, "Oh, he's all right."

"Is he harsh with you?" persisted his father.

"No," Mathew answered truthfully, but neglected to add that McDonnell seemed to have forgotten his new apprentice existed.

3

MATHEW'S FIRST
PAMPHLET

FOR TWO YEARS Mathew enjoyed the company of his fellow apprentice. He also had been accepted by the dwellers in the Liberties, and had made friends with them. In all this time, however, McDonnell never mellowed. He was a harsh master. No matter how industrious and careful the boys were in their work, never once did he give them a word of praise.

One evening at supper, Mrs. McDonnell heard her husband swear and heap abuse upon his apprentices for some work he had spoiled himself. When he had picked up his hat and left to pour out his troubles to his cronies at the pub, she consoled the boys in her rough way.

"Pay him no mind, me lads," she said from the doorway where she watched her husband hustling down the lane. After a moment, she added over her shoulder, "The saying of a few kind words would kill him, that one, but he doesn't mean what he says, not by half."

The boys knew that the printer did not earn enough money to support his family. The thirty guineas he had received for Mathew's apprenticeship were almost gone. It was no surprise when McDonnell agreed to do the printing for another bookseller by the name of Wogan, a brute and a bully, who would charge into the shop, his red hair standing on end, and demand that his work be put on the press as soon as he brought it in. Many times he browbeat McDonnell and neither Tom nor Mathew was able to cope with him.

Wogan's apprentice, John O'Boyle, had learned bullying tactics from his employer. When he saw that neither boy could stand up to Wogan, he tried the same methods on them. One morning he swaggered into the shop and harshly scolded Tom for some incompleted work.

When Tom protested, O'Boyle punched him in the nose and Tom hit back. Although smaller, Tom was a better fighter, and in a few minutes O'Boyle called quits and left the shop, saying Tom would be sorry.

"Now I've done it," moaned Tom, while he tried to pull his torn shirt together. "What will McDonnell do when he hears?"

"You'll probably get a caning, but you should be used to them by now," said Mathew. "I'd say it was worth it."

But to the surprise of both, McDonnell thought the fight a huge joke, even saying he wished he could have seen it. He never did like that rapscallion.

He was still laughing when Mathew glanced out the door and saw Wogan striding down the lane, his bushy eyebrows drawn together in a way that spelled disaster for someone. The angry man burst into the shop and brushed Mathew aside with such force that the boy sprawled on the floor.

"Where is that ruffian McMahon?" he bellowed. He spied Tom and shouted, "You coward, to attack my poor apprentice without cause!"

Although Tom insisted that O'Boyle had struck the first blow, Wogan demanded a public apology.

"What for, sir?" asked Tom. "I'm sorry if he's hurt, but unless O'Boyle apologizes for starting the brawl, I won't apologize for hitting him."

Shaking a finger under Tom's nose, Wogan shouted, "John O'Boyle will never apologize!"

"Then neither will I, sir." Tom walked to the rear of the shop and picked up a rag to clean the press.

Wogan strode from the shop and within half an hour, O'Boyle returned and stuttered that he was challenging McMahon to a duel. In a daze, Tom watched the boy leave the shop.

McDonnell was indignant. "I never thought Wogan would be imbecile enough to go to such a length in this business," he said. He pointed a forefinger at Tom's nose and said, "You won't go to the meeting place. I forbid it." Raising his voice, he shouted, "I forbid it, do you hear?" Then as he relaxed, he continued with a smirk, "He can't fight you, if you're not there, can he?"

When the angry Wogan once again came to the shop, McDonnell, for once, stood up for his boys, and told the man to find someone his own size if he wanted to pick a fight.

The incident was over, but Mathew could not rid his mind of the thought of the duel. What wickedness to risk human life over some slight wrong, whether real or fancied. Suppose Tom had been killed or cruelly maimed for life!

One day when his friend was on an errand and McDonnell

out, Mathew took a sheet of paper and wrote his thoughts on duels. As an illustration, he used the challenge to Tom.

Mathew thought the essay good and decided to send it to the *Hibernian journal.* Somebody had to raise his voice against such evil. Much to his surprise, this, his first piece, was accepted and published.

Once more Wogan stormed down the alley. He showed the article to McDonnell and demanded to know who had written it. Mathew confessed that he was the author. This time McDonnell did not side with his boys.

"You young idiot," he shouted, "who gave you the privilege of writing to the newspapers about Mr. Wogan?" He pounded the table before which he was standing and shouted, "He's a friend of mine, don't forget it."

Wogan stood beside McDonnell, and glared at the apprentice.

Mathew stood as erect as he could, and dared to protest: "I only told the truth."

At his words, Wogan raised his arm to strike the boy. Tom, who had been standing quietly behind Mathew, stepped between them, fists clenched at his side.

"You see," said Wogan as he dropped his arm and turned to McDonnell. "That one is a defiant bully. I warned you before."

"Pack your things and go, boy. I'm through with you!" McDonnell shouted in a vain effort to satisfy Wogan.

Mathew's protest that it was he who was at fault, did no good. Tom was dismissed and disappeared from Mathew's life forever.

For Mathew, life at McDonnell's was very dull indeed without Tom's company. Since he was now so much alone and had been encouraged by the publication of his first essay, he thought of writing others. He felt he had to write on a topic of great concern, and he knew of nothing in Ireland of greater distress to the people than the Penal Laws with their galling restrictions. Obsessed with the injustice of the Penal Laws, he read everything he could on the subject, then wrote a pamphlet on *The Urgent Necessity of the Repeal of the Penal Code against Roman Catholics.* He intended to print and sell the pamphlet himself, and with a true sense of showmanship, he printed and distributed fiery leaflets announcing its publication.

But this met with a reception he had not expected. A Catholic association, which had been formed to better conditions was, to Mathew's horror, leaning over backward to avoid real trouble with the British. This association, fearing that the British would accuse them of backing the pamphlet, and that any slight gain they had already made would be lost, offered forty pounds for the discovery of the author.

News traveled fast through the Liberties. The reward had scarcely been posted before Mathew heard about it. That night, he sat on his straw pallet and tried to consider what he should do. If he were discovered and dragged to jail, his family would be disgraced. He must tell his father of his rash act.

Mathew thought Saturday evening would never come. At last he was free to go home. For the first time he was afraid as he hurried through the Liberties. Would someone discover he was the man with a price on his head? He glanced fearfully down each street until he came to Redmond's Hill.

At home he found the usual feast ready for him, but he had lost his appetite. When his father mentioned that he seemed to be only toying with the food on his plate, the youth replied that he wasn't hungry. He rose from the table to stand silently by the mantle, his back to the fire. After the dishes had been cleared away, the conversation was resumed.

For several minutes, Mathew talked with his parents then brought the subject around to the furor. He took from his pocket the leaflet which advertised the pamphlet, and showed it to his father, saying, "Father, don't you think there is a lot of commotion abroad about a pamphlet no one has yet read in its entirety?"

Mr. Carey glanced at the leaflet and passed it on to his wife, then said that although he had heard about it, he had not seen a copy. Were they all over the Liberties? As he leaned back in his chair and folded his arms, he remarked that he supposed hotheads were necessary, but they often stirred up more trouble than they were worth, and it was certainly true in the case of this man—whoever he was.

Mathew asked, "Have you read the pamphlet, Father?"

"No, and neither have you," answered his father mildly.

With eyes lowered, Mathew told him quietly, "I have."

"Where?" his father demanded as he sat up straight in his chair.

"At the print shop," replied Mathew.

Mr. Carey leaped from his chair, and paced back and forth. He paused before Mathew and said that he didn't know McDonnell went in for that kind of printing, and did Mathew know the author?

"McDonnell knows nothing about this. I am the author," Mathew answered with a wan smile.

Mrs. Carey gasped, and her husband sank into his chair, stunned.

"But the pamphlet does not urge sedition," insisted

Mathew. "Besides it hasn't all been printed yet. Part is still in type. I can't see why there is so much fuss."

His father looked at him for a long moment, then remarked that the consequences of Mathew's folly would not be very pleasant. The boy should suffer for his foolhardiness, but he guessed that was what fathers were for—to help.

"Well have to decide what is to be done," he said thoughtfully. "You say some of this is still in type?"

Mathew nodded dumbly.

"That is where we must begin," said Mr. Carey, as he rose and headed for the door. "Come on, Mathew, well go to the shop."

Father and son walked the streets in silence. Rain fell, and the city had become hushed as though it were a part of the conspiracy. Even the revelers passed by quickly and quietly. McDonnell was out and no one paid any attention to the two as they entered the shop and lit a lamp.

Once there, Mr. Carey stood by and watched Mathew uncover the forms, unlock them, and distribute the type. Then he climbed to the loft, and brought from their hiding place the unsold copies of the first section of the pamphlet and tied them up to give them to his father. With the large package under his arm, Mr. Carey prepared to leave, but gave Mathew strict instructions not to set foot out the door until he was sent for. He could hide in the shop in complete safety, for it was unlikely that even McDonnell would set foot inside the establishment on Saturday night or Sunday. The boy stood forlornly in the doorway and watched his father trudge down the street, then he went up to bed, but not to sleep.

On Monday, Mr. Carey went to speak to the members of the Catholic association and came right to the point.

"Gentlemen," he said, "the pamphlet was written by my son Mathew, who regrets his impetuous act."

On hearing Mr. Carey's statement, the officers straightened in their chairs and their faces hardened. Every eye was fastened on Mr. Carey as he went on to say that Mathew had distributed the type for the second section, and that he, personally, would burn the unsold copies of the first section, if the group would withdraw the charges.

"After all," he said, "he is but a thoughtless boy."

When Mr. Carey had finished, a violent discussion was carried on across the table. Everyone wanted to talk at once. Even if the act were not malicious, it endangered the good of all, someone insisted. Every hothead on the Island would be taking up his pen, if an example were not made of this heedless youth, said another.

With an increasing feeling of distress, Mr. Carey listened to the cold-blooded debate that affected his son. By the time he rose from the conference table, he knew that Mathew could expect no mercy from these men. The boy was rash and deserved a reprimand, but he was not a criminal. He must be shielded from such viciousness.

Late that night, Mr. Carey sent his son John to take Mathew to the home of a friend who lived near the quays. Since he wanted to keep Mathew's whereabouts a secret if possible, instead of rousing the McDonnell family, John shot pebbles at the loft window to arouse his brother. Mathew crept downstairs to walk with John quickly and quietly through the dark streets.

On the way, John explained that it was necessary to leave Ireland for a time and that their father was laying plans.

After Mathew had been hiding for five days, a packet came into port. The captain was a friend of Mr. Carey. He agreed to take the boy as a passenger and land him safely in France.

A few minutes before sailing time, Mr. Carey came down to the dock with Mathew who was limping badly. They stood for a moment at the gangplank while the father embraced the boy, then pressed a purse with a few guineas into his son's hand.

"God bless you, my boy, and do stay out of trouble," cautioned Mr. Carey, his hand resting on his son's shoulder.

"I'll try, Father," Mathew answered soberly.

Mr. Carey took a paper from his pocket and gave it to his son.

"This letter will introduce you to a friend of Father Betagh's who is at present at Passy, near Paris. Go to him," said his father. "I understand he is a kind man, and will do all he can for you."

"Yes, Father," murmured the boy.

"Both your mother and I are greatly distressed that there is nothing else we can do but let you go. Be sure to drop us a line often, and let us know how you are doing."

Their farewells were interrupted by the mate, who shouted, "All aboard, the tide is running."

"God bless you, my boy," said his father. Mathew hugged him swiftly, then hurried up the gangplank, trying to hold back his tears.

From the deck, he saluted the lonely figure on the dock, and regretted that he was forced to flee and leave his father to face the unpleasantness caused by his own folly.

4
EXILE AND RETURN

"GOING ADVENTURING, eh, lad?" the mate asked Mathew Carey who was leaning on the ship's rail looking shoreward.

"In a manner of speaking," replied Mathew, straining for a last glimpse of Dublin. "I'm escaping from persecution."

"Ye'll not be the first of your countrymen to do that," remarked the mate, slapping the boy on the shoulder.

Mathew smiled gratefully at the man, then once more turned to stare at the Wicklow Hills as they faded into the dusk. It was not long before the packet reached the open sea, and Mathew, suddenly seasick, staggered to the cabin where he found a hard bench to lie on.

An hour later, having grown more accustomed to the motion of the ship, the boy found strength enough to glance at the address on the letter his father had given him. It read:

To: His Excellency, Benjamin Franklin.
Passy, France.

Never, even in his wildest dreams, had he pictured himself, an apprentice to a poor printer, fleeing to France to Dr. Franklin, the American ambassador. The thought of McDonnell, angry at his disappearance, stomping around the shop, swearing and uttering curses on all ungrateful apprentices, caused Mathew to grin wanly.

Feeling a little better, he dragged himself to the upper deck where he once more met the mate who pointed to a coil of rope on which he could sit.

"Fresh air always helps," the mate said kindly, then, giving way to his curiosity, asked, "Friends meeting you in France?"

"No, sir, I'm entirely on my own," said Mathew with dignity, hoping to appear older than his nineteen years. With more confidence than he felt, he added, "I'm a printer and will find a job."

"Do you speak French?" asked the mate.

"That I do," replied Mathew, recalling the hours he had spent studying French, not realizing that one day he would need to know the language if he wanted as much as a crust of bread.

On landing in France, Mathew took the stage for Paris and on his arrival spent a day wandering around the streets. The beautiful city, with its many bridges crossing the Seine, made him homesick for his beloved Dublin and the arches spanning the Liffey. Realizing he must find work, he inquired how to reach Passy, and was told that he could go there by coach. He learned also that Benjamin Franklin had set up a press at Passy to print and distribute his dispatches from America. Could he hope that Dr. Franklin would employ him?

As the coach bounced along the dusty road to Passy, Mathew braced himself in a corner and wondered if the great man would receive him. He was too worried even to notice the barren, frost-covered fields through which they passed on the way. Within an hour he arrived at Passy.

To his astonishment, when he entered Franklin's office, Mathew found the great man sitting alone at a table, balancing a column of figures. While he stood waiting, he kept his eyes on the sturdy old man in brown wool breeches and coat, with gray shoulder-length hair forming a fringe around his bald pate, and square-lensed glasses resting on the tip of his nose.

When Dr. Franklin became aware of the young man standing by the table, he pushed his glasses to the top of his head, looked at the youth with interest, and said:

"Eh? How long have I kept you standing there, my friend?"

"Not long, sir," answered Mathew. Put at ease by the old man's warm smile, he continued, "I have a letter of introduction, sir."

Dr. Franklin took the letter, indicating the chair near the table. Mathew sat on the edge of the chair, anxiously trying to figure out the meaning of the raised eyebrows and little exclamations of surprise. At last the old man looked up and said:

"So you would incite the Irish to revolt! A regular firebrand, eh?"

"Not really, sir."

Ignoring Mathew's protest, Franklin continued: "You're a bit young to beard the lion. Yet, on second thought, it took a David to fell Goliath."

Knowing that he merely had been impetuous, Mathew squirmed under Franklin's gaze as the old man went on: "It's youth we need to carry on the fight. We old ones lack the strength."

"If I may be so bold to disagree, sir," Mathew said in all sincerity, "it's the wisdom of age we need to control the folly of youth."

"You Irish with your blarney," laughed Franklin. "Go find the master printer and tell him I said to take you on."

"Oh, thank you, sir," began Mathew, but Franklin, once more deep in figures, waved the youth to the rear of the shop. There he found a dozen men and boys, each busy about his own task. An apprentice, staggering under a bundle of paper, indicated the foreman with a jerk of his head.

Assuming that Mathew was a journeyman, that is, an experienced printer, the master put him to setting up a page of a report. Many times Mathew blessed Tom McMahon and the things he taught him, for McDonnell never had showed him so much as how to set up a line of type.

Mathew worked very hard and carefully for Dr. Franklin. By watching the other typesetters and pressmen, he learned much about his trade. Rarely did Franklin find an opportunity to come into the shop, but each time he did, he spoke to the men with friendliness. Mathew felt that his employer was a great and kindly man.

One day Dr. Franklin sent for Mathew to come to the front of the shop. When he arrived, he found the good doctor in conversation with a handsome young Frenchman who was wearing with ease the satins and fine laces of the nobility.

"Mathew," said Dr. Franklin to the youth who hesitated in the doorway, "come here, my boy. I want to present you to the Marquis de Lafayette."

The Marquis acknowledged Mathew's awkward bob with a sweeping bow that would have served for royalty.

"I've been most anxious to meet you, Monsieur Carey," he said. "Would you do me the honor of speaking with me for a few minutes?"

Mathew managed to stammer, "Delighted, sir." Dr. Franklin beamed. "Anything you can do for the Marquis, I would consider a favor, my boy." Mathew took off his apron and slipped into his coat. The laces of the Frenchman and the somber woolens of the young printer were in sharp contrast as they walked across the road to the inn. Mathew knew all about Lafayette and his interest in America, and had heard of his recall to help France fight her old enemy, England. What could this aristocrat and soldier want of him? the lad wondered. He was not kept long in ignorance.

The Marquis led the way to his room and offered the

youth a chair before the large fireplace in which a great log was burning. Pulling up his chair, Lafayette sat facing the young Irishman. He leaned forward to offer Mathew some tobacco, saying, "I became accustomed to smoking when I was fighting in America last year."

Never having used tobacco, Mathew thought it best to refuse.

"Monsieur Carey," began the Marquis, "Dr. Franklin tells me that you are no friend of the British."

"The British have done dreadful things to my country, sir," Mathew returned. "How could I be a friend to them?"

"Maybe, then, you could tell me how well the Irish are organized politically and how many we could depend on should we invade Ireland," Lafayette said eagerly.

So that was the reason for this strange call. The Marquis, in common with the English, had thought him, a young apprentice, a mouthpiece for a rebellious group of Irishmen. When he had sat in the back of McDonnell's shop writing his pamphlet, Mathew had not realized the interpretation that would be put on his work. He'd have to try to explain his case.

"I wish I could, sir, but I know naught of any organization save that whose members have caused me to be an exile, a price upon my head, for the crime of trying to defend them." He shook his head sadly. "And, moreover, those rascals I sought to help denounced me as a meddler and a villain."

The Marquis shifted the log. "Then the Irish have no fight left in them?" he asked, his tone betraying his disappointment.

"I would not say that," protested Mathew earnestly. "I do say that in their hearts they can't help but hate the King, but if they be organized, I know naught of it. I stand before you, sir, a poor fellow brought into trouble because of the thoughtless words he put into print."

Knowing the interview was at an end, Mathew got to his feet. The Marquis rose, clapped him on the shoulder, and said, "It's enough, my friend, to know that the Irish are finding the spirit to rebel against their overlords, even though it be in individual cases."

Mathew never forgot this, his first meeting with the man who so ardently believed in and fought for freedom.

In another month, the work in the shop began to slacken off, so Mathew was not surprised when after supper one night a few weeks later Dr. Franklin asked him to walk in the garden. Each plant interested the American ambassador.

"Look, Mathew, see how the violets are coming up. It's spring again." Then, glancing at his companion, he said, "You've been with me for about two months, my boy. I like your industry and interest, but as you see, my need for this shop is drawing to a close."

"Yes, sir, I've noticed the work is slackening," said Mathew, feeling once more forlorn and alone.

Dr. Franklin continued in his offhand manner: "I've learned that Didot le Jeune is printing some books in English and is in need of a printer. Would you like to go to work for him?"

"Didot le Jeune, sir?" Mathew gasped, stopping short. "He's the best printer on the continent."

"That's right, my boy," said his employer giving his arm an affectionate pat. "Go with him and you will learn your trade thoroughly."

"Dr. Franklin, you have been more than kind to me, a stranger," Mathew burst out gratefully.

"You have earned your chance, my boy. I have great faith in you," Franklin answered.

"Someday, sir, I hope to visit your country to see its wonders for myself," Mathew said.

"Do better than that, come join us," suggested Dr. Franklin.

A few days later, Mathew took the stage back to Paris along the same road he had traveled two months earlier. Then, he had been homesick and hunted, and apprehensive about his reception. How different was this return trip made through the green fields brilliant with spring flowers. He was going to work for the best printer in Europe, assured of his welcome, the road having been smoothed by the remarkable American diplomat.

Arriving in Paris, Mathew stood in awe before the large plant owned by the Didot family. Having gathered enough courage to go into the printing office, he presented his letter from Dr. Franklin and was accepted without question.

For about a year Mathew labored with Didot. He found the work hard and exacting, but at last he had learned to be a real printer.

The young man spent every free moment exploring Paris. There were scarcely any sections into which curiosity did not lead him. He saw the rich and the poor, visited churches and theaters, and ate all of the strange food offered to him. The colorful satins and laces of the young men of fashion interested him, and as soon as he had saved enough money, he changed his dull woolens for brighter plumage, even to the purchase of a powdered wig.

At last a letter came from Mathew's father telling him that the anger against him had died, and that it would be safe to come home. Mathew asked Monsieur Francois Didot when he could be spared.

His employer told him that within a month the last English book would be off the press, and there would be a few months before they would need another English printer.

Within a fortnight, Mathew and his trunk of fine clothes were on a packet bound for Ireland, an eventful and useful year behind him. Looking down at his cutaway coat, Mathew thought that he soon would be changing it for the coarse woolens he would wear when he returned to McDonnell's, for he still owed the man a year's service. He recalled with distaste the filthy shop in the Liberties, but there was nothing for it but to give McDonnell his due.

After a smooth voyage, the packet came slowly up the Liffey. Mathew stood on deck impatiently, watching the ship nose into the dock. As soon as he could, he hurried ashore. He took a carriage which, in a few minutes, turned into the familiar street with its rows of brick homes, each with red geraniums blooming in window boxes. As the carriage stopped at the door, a brief shower was chased by the sun, which turned every blade of grass into a setting for raindrop diamonds. Mathew hurried up the steps and pounded the knocker. The door was flung open and his mother hugged him tightly, the rest of the family crowding around him, plying him with questions.

That night at dinner when talk had quieted a bit, his father remarked casually, "I have a surprise for you, my boy."

Mathew looked at his father, wondering what the news could be. Helping himself to a piece of fish, Mr. Carey continued, "I've purchased your apprenticeship from McDonnell."

Mathew froze, a forkful of potatoes halfway to his mouth.

Recovering from the shock, he gasped in relief, slowly returning his fork to his plate. After regaining his voice, he said, "Thank you, Father, I've dreaded returning to the shop and days of idleness."

His father's face in the flickering candlelight took on a bottled-up look—that of a man bursting with news, but trying to be nonchalant in telling it. "Days of idleness there won't be, my boy, if you agree to what I have in mind for you," said his father.

"And what is that, Father?" asked Mathew.

Leaning back with his hands on the arms of his chair, Mr. Carey said, "I have found a place for you on the staff of the *Freeman's Journal*. Does that interest you?"

Mathew was amazed at his father's question. The *Freeman's Journal* defended the Irish cause as loudly as possible. Surely his father was aware of this, and yet, knowing his son to be a hothead, he was giving him the opportunity to print his views. Mathew could not hope for a better opening. Of course he wanted the position!

His dinner forgotten, he sat dreaming of the things he would like to print. His father broke into his reverie with a word of caution.

"Be careful what you write, my boy."

"I'll write only the truth," promised Mathew.

"No one can ask for more," answered Mr. Carey. He then turned the conversation to happenings in the family while Mathew was away.

The following Monday, Mathew joined the staff of the *Freeman's Journal*. In the course of his duties during the next two years, he contributed many articles fostering the desire of the Irish for freedom.

His work must have pleased his father, for on the 13th of October, 1783, that astounding man called Mathew into his study. Asking his son to be seated, Mr. Carey questioned him closely on the cost of running a newspaper and the money necessary. Putting pen and paper before the young man, he asked to have the expenses itemized for him. Mathew, humoring his father, wrote out all the costs involved and totaled them for him. Mr. Carey glanced at the sum, and, rummaging in a drawer of his desk, he drew out a leather bag, from which he dumped gold pieces in a pile between them.

"Count them, son," he said, "I think you will find enough there to establish a paper." Without another word, he rose from his chair and hurried out of the room, leaving Mathew staring at the coins in utter disbelief.

At last Mathew could really fight for Irish freedom. As the owner and editor of a journal, he was in complete control of the views expressed in its pages.

Busy days followed for the young editor. He had to find a shop, presses, and a printer, for he would be far too busy managing the journal to take time to feed a press. At last he found a suitable shop on Abbey Street. His brother James offered to work with him awhile.

Shortly the *Volunteer's Journal*, as he called his newspaper, was in print, and before long became the most widely read paper in Ireland. Its purpose, the owner stated, was to defend the commerce, manufactures, and political rights of Ireland against Great Britain. Its violent and angry tone fitted the temper of the people of the time. Mathew Carey, now a popular and sporting figure around town, played on the sensitive feelings of his readers.

No matter how trivial the slight to the Irish, he made capital of it. He realized, though, that neither he nor the people could do a thing to improve conditions. Any change in the Irish situation must come from the men who sat in Parliament, and the members of the Irish Parliament were merely the mouthpiece of the British Parliament. Little help could be expected from these men.

5

ESCAPE

MATHEW CAREY met his literary friends at Dick's Coffee House, where nightly they discussed the members of the Irish Parliament. Somehow, those timid men must be exposed for the cowardly way they submitted to the dictates of the British. The young editor filled the *Volunteers Journal* with his opinions and those of his friends. In each issue of the newspaper, he wrote an article bolder than the one before.

The issue of April 5, 1784, carried an attack on John Foster, the Premier of Parliament, and was illustrated by a woodcut that pictured the Premier dangling from a gibbet. Mathew was pleased at the comment caused by the article, not realizing that he had goaded Parliament too far.

On April 7, he sent his brother James to the House of Commons to gather news for the forthcoming issue of the *Journal.* James relaxed on a bench in the public gallery, half listening to the business of Parliament, then he jumped to his feet as he heard the Premier announce:

"This body is offering a reward for the apprehension of Mathew Carey . . ."

Openmouthed, James heard the Premier drone on, ". . . for publishing in his paper a daring, false, scandalous and seditious libel on the proceeding of this house."

Before the Premier had finished, James was out of the building and frantically hailing a carriage. He urged the driver to even greater speed as they careened off Essex Bridge, and galloped toward Sackville Street. Scarcely had the coachman reined in the horse on Abbey Street, when James jumped out of the carriage and rushed into the shop, calling Mathew to come at once.

Mathew reached for his hat and followed his brother into the carriage, not knowing what calamity had befallen them. James directed they be taken to Skinner's Row, then in reply to Mathew's demand to know what happened, said:

"John Foster has put a price on your head. I'm taking you to Dick's Coffee House. You can hide in the back room."

Mathew was at first amused that he had really annoyed Parliament enough to hurt, then asked how much he was worth this time! His second thought was that it was cowardly to run away from these men. "Let's go to them, James, then we can collect the reward," he said laughing heartily.

Before Mathew could order the driver to turn around, James put a detaining hand on his brother's shoulder. He inquired if Mathew intended to let Parliament think that he'd run to them when they snapped their fingers.

"I hadn't thought of that," said Mathew and allowed James to have his way.

In the meantime, Mr. L'Estrange, the Sergeant at Arms for Parliament, received his orders to produce Mathew Carey. He and his men went to the shop in Abbey Street, but their quarry was not there and none of the workmen knew where the editor had gone.

The officer looked from one impassive face to another, and remarked, "You wouldn't tell me if you knew."

There was no answer, but the sly looks exchanged by Mathew's loyal workmen proved him correct.

Since it was obvious from the disordered state of the editor's desk that Mathew had left in a hurry, the constables decided to play a waiting game, for Carey could be holed up in any one of a hundred places, Mr. L'Estrange said. He had friends all over the city, even in the Liberties.

"He'll be back in a few days," the Sergeant at Arms added. "In the meantime, we'll set an all-night watch on the shop."

This plan was kept so quiet that no word of a search or watch on the shop came to Mathew's ears. He thought that John Foster had made a gesture without any serious intention of carrying it out.

Since there were important papers in his files that Mathew needed if he were to continue his campaign against Parliament, he became impatient about getting them. Without mentioning his plan to anyone, he stole out of his hiding place before dawn on Sunday morning. No one saw him as he entered his shop, the whole city being asleep—no one but the guard who stood in the shadow of the opposite doorway.

Cautiously, Mathew entered his shop and hastened from file to file to gather up the required letters. He nearly had completed the task when he felt a rush of fresh air and knew that the door had opened noiselessly. Over his shoulder, he saw the bailiff who blocked the exit as he held out a warrant for Mathew's arrest. Rain had begun to fall, and as the surprised editor was marched out to a waiting carriage, he remarked ruefully that it was most kind of the man to see that he did not have to walk home in the wet!

Instead of taking Mathew to jail, the Sergeant at Arms kept the prisoner in his own home and would not allow him to get in touch with anyone. The young man's family and friends were frantic. No one had seen him leave his hiding place, and the arrest at the shop happened so quickly and quietly that there were no witnesses. For eight days his brothers inquired at every prison in fear of his arrest, even dreading foul play. Their search ended on April 19, when Mathew was called before Parliament on charges of libel.

Denied counsel, the young man stood alone before the dais. With head thrown back and chin thrust forward, he gazed steadily at the Premier. Mr. Foster put question after question to him, but he refused to answer. To each query, he merely said, "This is a civil suit, and must be tried by the Lord Mayor. Parliament has no right to try me."

No matter what line of reasoning they followed, it could not be established that Mathew Carey was legally a prisoner of Parliament. After he had heard all the arguments, Mr. Foster said that the calendar of cases was too full to waste time on this man, and ordered the accused held in Newgate prison until Parliament had finished more pressing business.

Mathew was elated, knowing that he had won his point and that John Foster was merely trying to save face. After a mocking bow to the members of Parliament, he allowed the guards, who surrounded him as though they feared he would be spirited away, to lead him off to prison.

In Newgate, Mathew made the usual financial arrangements with his jailers. It was the custom of those times for a well-to-do prisoner to offer a sum of money to the jailers and in return have good food brought in and the privilege of as many visitors as he wished. Mathew's friends came daily to dine with him on pheasant and great loins of beef. They stayed to play cards and strum on lutes. All joined in to fill the pages of the *Volunteers journal* with stories of the martyrdom of its distinguished editor. So well did they do their work, that his persecution became a topic of conversation in Europe and even in America.

Although Mathew's days in prison were filled with fun and laughter, both he and his family were relieved when on May 14, still ignoring the case, Parliament adjourned. The following day, the Lord Mayor set Mathew free.

His brothers met him at the prison gate, and they drove to Redmond's Hill where his parents were awaiting him. Mathew thought the scarlet geraniums in their boxes never looked brighter, and his mother, standing in the doorway, never looked sweeter.

After a fine dinner, the ladies went into the drawing room, leaving the men to talk. Mathew rose from the table and limped to the window, pulling aside the heavy curtain to glance at the guards spying on him from across the street. They, along with one at the rear of the house, had followed him home from Newgate prison. Mathew let the drapery fall into place, and returned to the table to listen to the conversation.

"You are aware, my boy, that your present state is only a reprieve," said his father, looking at him gravely. "As soon as Parliament convenes in the fall, you will be indicted once again."

Mathew realized this all too well, and also knew that the Attorney General had dismissed the all Irish Grand Jury. When he came up for trial in the fall, Parliament would have taken on the duties of prosecutor and jury as well as judge. There was no doubt that he would be convicted.

Mr. Carey said that his advice would be for Mathew to go away, and since the exile would be for a long time, his son should choose well the place he would like to make his home.

Mathew agreed to go away, but where? After a taste of publishing, he did not want to return to the trade of printing, even though he knew he would be welcomed by Didot le Jeune in Paris. Benjamin Franklin and his invitation to "join us" came to mind. He also recalled the enthusiasm with which Lafayette had spoken of America.

"If I must go," he said, "I'll go to America."

His father agreed that America was a wise choice, but added that, to his regret, he had no funds available at the moment to offer aid.

James offered to buy the *Volunteers Journal*. "Do you consider five hundred pounds a fair price?" he asked, explaining he could pay twenty-five guineas immediately and the remainder in three installments at six months' intervals. Mathew accepted gladly and leaned forward to shake hands on the bargain.

Since they had decided on escape, the Careys made careful plans. They knew that somehow the guards must be outwitted. Mathew was to harry them as much as possible, and throw them off the track, a task he performed with great glee.

He took lodgings near the quays and all summer kept the guards guessing what he would do next. Wherever he went, they had to follow.

Not only did Mathew go out at all hours, but he also had visitors at unexpected times. His family and friends came to see him often, but, by far, his most frequent guest was his sister Margaret. She called with her husband, and sometimes with her mother, but more often one of her brothers was her escort. The deputies came to know Mrs. Margaret Burke very well and faithfully noted each call she made. Sometimes she even nodded to them. One man remarked to his companion that each night his wife asked him to describe Mrs. Burke's costume. Thank goodness she always wore a cloak so all he had to remember were the hats, and they were bad enough.

On September 7, Mrs. Burke and her brother John called on Mathew early in the afternoon and stayed a long time. When they left, the guards noted their departure.

"Mrs. Burke must be taking a trip," remarked one to another. "She's wearing her traveling cloak and hood. I must remember to tell my wife that the hood is so deep it completely hides her face."

The men idly watched her walk with her brother John to the carriage at the head of the street. "Wonder how she hurt her foot," commented one of the men. "Did you notice how she is limping?"

His companion straightened up and bellowed, "Limping, did you say? That was Carey! Come on!" They ran up the street calling "Stop!" at the top of their lungs. Mathew's neighbors, who had seen the couple enter their carriage and drive off at a gallop, made every effort to slow down the two men. Children began a frantic game of tag, running around the men who were pounding up the street. The flower vendor overturned her basket, and the passersby, who stooped to help her pick up her wares, blocked the way. By the time the men reached the corner, there was no carriage in sight and no one knew which way it had gone. Long ago, the Irish had learned ways of obstructing a constable when he was in pursuit of one of their own.

Chagrined, the guards drove to the home of Mr. L'Estrange to tell of their failure and ask what was to be done.

"Find him!" barked the Sergeant at Arms, and prepared to join in the search.

In the meantime, the carriage jolted right along, turning and doubling to escape possible pursuers. Within a few blocks, the carriage stopped beside a farmer's cart piled high with produce, driven by his brother Tom. Mathew scrambled out of the coach and up beside Tom, who immediately set off for the docks, while John drove in another direction.

Elated by the escape, Mathew gave Tom a playful push and said laughingly, "You make a fine farmer, Tom."

"You're not out of trouble yet," Tom said as he glanced behind them. "Hold your head down, and pray we can carry our plans through."

They drove on the dock beside the packet *America,* which was taking on supplies. The supercargo, the officer in charge of this operation, was checking each item as it was carried aboard. When the produce cart drove up, he directed the stevedores to unload the bags from the cart.

Mathew slipped out of his sister's petticoats and cloak, beneath which he wore the dark woolens of a laborer. He clapped his brother on the back and said with affection, "Good-by, Tom, and God bless you.

Then according to plan, he shouldered a sack of potatoes from the cart. With lowered head, he walked up the gangplank.

The supercargo ordered him to carry his sack to the galley. There Mathew met the mate who led the way to the hold and pointed out an empty space behind some barrels. After having carefully concealed the young man, the mate turned to leave, saying, "As soon as we're at sea, I'll be down for you. Just you rest easy, sir."

Mathew tried to make himself comfortable in his cramped quarters. The space was so small that he had to sit with his knees drawn up so that his chin rested on them. Although startled at first by odd creaking noises and scurrying rats, he settled down to wait, laughing silently at the smoothness with which his escape had been carried out. He knew he was not yet out of danger, nor would he be, until the ship was under way. Suspicion would most certainly center on the ships, especially this one bound for America. His pursuers might be searching her now. At a scrambling noise, he stiffened, then relaxed. It was only a rat. Then he felt a slight motion. The ship was slowly pulling away from the dock. Mathew sighed and tried to shift the position of his cramped legs.

Relief quickly turned to fear, for the *America* had scarcely left her berth and swung around to go downriver, before Mathew heard the scraping and rattling of the anchor chain as it was payed out. The slowly moving ship stopped, then swayed gently with the tide. Could the searchers have trailed him? In a few minutes, he heard someone open the hatch, and daylight streamed in.

Ponderous footsteps sounded on the ladder, followed by a light, quick step. Someone was saying, "Mr. L'Estrange, I'll conduct you through the ship myself, but I must protest this delay. Your men have already searched once and found nothing amiss."

"You'll not sail until I'm satisfied, Captain Keiler," Mr. L'Estrange replied in a tone so offensive that Mathew, himself, longed to answer the man.

The captain, however, chose to ignore the rudeness, and went on to explain that the cargo must be packed solidly, lest it shift in a storm and the ship founder.

Mr. L'Estrange interrupted the captain, saying testily that he could see for himself that there was no place to hide there. He then requested a look at the passengers, and stated that it would not be wise to try to conceal a single one. The two men climbed the ladder, and the hold was left in darkness.

Mathew, crouching there, wondered how long it would be before he could stretch his legs. In a few minutes, the welcome sound of scraping chain came to his straining ears. At last, he felt the motion of the ship under way!

Wicklow Hills had dropped from sight before the mate came below to help the fugitive from his cramped quarters. Awkwardly, Mathew climbed the steep ladder to the deck where he was greeted heartily by Captain Keiler.

"We had a close call, Mr. Carey," he said, "but our troubles are over. We're at sea."

Then the captain took Mathew to the passenger's cabin to introduce him to his shipmates, saying that he was the culprit causing their delay. Curious, the passengers plied Mathew with questions, to which the young man replied willingly, making the whole escapade sound like some huge joke. The swinging lamps were lit before Mathew had finished his tale.

That evening at supper, Mathew looked carefully at the group who would be his companions for the next two months. A young lady with dark curls escaping from under her cap was seated at the far side of the table. She glanced at him shyly. The trip might be pleasant after all, thought Mathew, smiling at her until he met the glare of her portly chaperone. His gaze then wandered the length of the table. Several of the young men evidently were emigrating like himself. One, a modestly dressed fellow who had been introduced as John Wallace, having seen the glare of the chaperone, grinned at him broadly. In contrast to Mr. Wallace were two men decked out in the latest fashion. One leaned forward and spoke of the boredom of such a long trip, then asked if anyone were interested in a game of cards. John Wallace said that if the play was for money, he was not interested.

"We play for modest stakes, or the game becomes uninteresting," said the man.

Mathew thought he was right and agreed to play cards

with them. Each night the little group sat around the cabin table, the swinging lamp throwing their faces first in gloom and then in glare. Mathew won consistently. Each morning he gleefully reported his winnings to John Wallace and urged him to join the game.

"Can't you see these men are sharpers?" asked his new-found friend one morning as they sat on barrels in the lee of the sails.

"If so, I'm beating them at their own game," replied Mathew. "I came aboard with twenty-five guineas in my pocket, which I have already doubled."

He went on to explain that at this rate he would be well prepared to establish a newspaper on his arrival in Philadelphia. His fortune would be made even before he had his first payment from his brother James.

"Do you know anyone in Philadelphia?" asked his friend.

"No, not really," replied Mathew. "Benjamin Franklin for whom I worked in Paris is still in France and does not expect to return for a year."

"Then I am better off than you," said Wallace and proudly produced a letter of introduction to General Washington, which Mathew read with awe. John hoped to secure a teaching position in Virginia, where Washington made his home.

Day after day, Mathew and John sat and watched blue sky merge with sea. Mathew had the sensation that the ship was the only thing moving in the world. During the whole voyage only one other ship was sighted. Mathew breathed a sigh of relief when it proved to be an American vessel and not an English man-of-war.

Mathew looked forward eagerly to the evenings and his phenomenal luck at cards. Toward the end of October, the captain dropped into the cabin and remarked that in about a week they should sight land. The sharpers glanced at one another, and that very night Mathew's luck changed. After several nights of continuous losses, Mathew came on deck one morning and stood dejectedly by the rail. John looked at him questioningly.

At last Mathew said, "You were right, John. Those men have won half my capital. Last night I withdrew from the game."

With their destination near, deep shipboard friendships evaporated, except for Mathew's attachment for John Wallace. Everyone but the two young men spent hours repacking their possessions. It had been a long hard voyage through storms and hurricanes, and no one regretted it was about to end.

The weather had turned cold. Sunday, the last day of October, carried a hint of snow. The ship came slowly up Delaware Bay and anchored to await the pilot who would take her up the river. The flaming red of the sumac and gold of the maples that lined the shore astounded Mathew as he watched for the pilot to come aboard. The whole shore line was aflame. Never had he seen such vividly colored trees. At last, the pilot's small craft came alongside the ship, but Mathew's face became grave, for the pilot climbed the ladder with great difficulty and staggered to the deck. Obviously the man was drunk.

As they sailed up the Delaware River, Mathew watched with concern the sinuous wake of the ship. Before long the *America* lurched, threw him off balance, and settled with a sound as though the bottom had scraped on rock.

Captain Keiler took charge, saying the vessel was on the Brandywine shoals. He calmed the fears of the passengers, called for volunteers to help, and with the combined efforts of passengers and crew, freed the ship. He anchored for the night, then early Monday morning, proceeded up the Delaware to bring his ship to dock at the end of Arch Street in Philadelphia.

6

EARLY DAYS IN PHILADELPHIA

IT WAS All Saints' Day when they came ashore, so Mathew Carey and John Wallace decided to go to church. The mate who heard them planning said, "You'll find a Catholic chapel by walking down Third Street until you come to Willing's Alley."

The young men moved up tree-lined Arch Street, looking for Third. Leaves were falling, and Mathew stooped to pick up a multicolored one. "Look, John," he said, "we have landed in a world of gold, emeralds, and rubies. Virginia cannot possibly offer as much beauty as Philadelphia. Change your mind and stay in the city," he coaxed.

John smiled and said, "No," as they turned down Third Street. They walked its cobbled length until they spied Willing's Alley and saw a few stragglers entering the church, a plain white structure with a cross on top. When they entered Mass had begun, so they slipped into the last pew.

After Mass, Mathew and John knelt while the parishioners left the church. They saw a flaxenhaired German followed by a child escorted by a slave. Others of the churchgoers could have been their neighbors back home. As they rose to leave, John nudged Mathew to make sure he saw a copper-faced Indian, with long braids, glide on soft, beaded moccasins out a side door.

The young men left the church and slowly retraced their steps through the city. John Wallace said he thought he should present his letter of introduction to General Washington, and then consider the best means of getting to Virginia. The two young men decided to stop at the Inn of St. George and the Dragon for a cup of coffee. When they inquired, the host told them General Washington had gone home to Mount Vernon.

"The stage leaves from this tavern tomorrow morning at four," said the innkeeper as he refilled their cups. "You better make a reservation now." Mathew sat, his mug of coffee before him, and waited for John to complete his plans. I will be lonely, Mathew thought, without the companionship of John Wallace.

When John returned, Mathew, pretending a gaiety he did not feel, rose and said, "Come, John. Now I must find a place to live."

The innkeeper overheard the remark and told Mathew of a friend, John Sutter on Water Street, who took boarders. Mathew found Mr. Sutter and engaged a room scarcely large enough to hold a narrow bed, a table for his washbowl, and a chair. The small window did, however, look onto the gardens behind the large houses on Front Street; there, chrysanthemums bloomed in profusion.

The next morning at four, Mathew went to the inn to bid his friend good-by. Both promised to write. The night turned gray while Mathew stood beside the innkeeper and watched the stage clatter off.

"Coffee is on the fire," said the host, shivering in the chill air.

Mathew went into the inn and sat for a long time, his mug of coffee before him. *What is to become of me?* he wondered.

To Mathew, in his fit of depression, every path to success seemed barred. He wanted to establish a newspaper, but because of his foolhardy gambling, he was almost penniless. Since he was a stranger in a new land, there was no one from whom he could borrow the money he needed. Should he accept defeat at once and take a job, or prepare for his venture while awaiting James's next payment for the paper? If he were to run a newspaper, what cause should he defend? These questions constantly came to mind as he walked the city streets.

To help decide his course of action, Mathew began attending many sessions of the State Assembly that was discussing whether or not the country needed a Constitution. For over a hundred years, America had been a group of independent colonies, later uniting into states. When danger threatened, the states formed a loose federation. The common cause of the Revolution brought them more closely together. The decision each of the thirteen states now had to make was whether they should unite under a central government, or continue to act independently.

Mathew heard the arguments for and against a Constitution

and wondered how anyone could want other than a strong central government. Here was a cause he could champion.

Now that he had a purpose, Mathew felt his energy return. He hastened to his room and sat down with pad and pencil to figure anew the cost of establishing a paper. Over a month had passed since he had landed and bid good-by to John Wallace. He reproached himself for having been idle so long. As he worked, he shivered, for it was cold and there was no fire in his room. But in spite of his discomfort, he determined to throw off his lethargy and act.

As Mathew sat pondering over his figures, he heard his landlord's footsteps on the stairs. He paid no attention, but when they stopped in the hall before his room and Mr. Sutter's fist came down hard on his door, Mathew jumped. "Come in," he called, glad for the interruption, although he did not care for the man.

Mr. Sutter opened the door and handed him a note sealed with a crest.

Mathew gaped at the letter in his hand, but made no effort to open it.

"Ye be Mathew Carey, be'nt ye?" asked Mr. Sutter, as he planted himself firmly in the doorway.

"Yes, yes," Mathew nodded with his eyes on the letter.

"Then, why don't ye open it, or can't ye read?" asked Mr. Sutter curiously.

Recovered somewhat from his surprise, Mathew broke the seal and looked at the signature. His face broke into a smile when he saw the note was from the Marquis de Lafayette, and that it was an invitation to call on him at the London Coffee House at four that day.

"Good news?" asked Mr. Sutter needlessly, for Mathew

had straightened his shoulders and his smile had widened to a grin.

"The best ever, my friend. Do you think your wife could press my ruffles?"

How could the Marquis have known where to find him? Mathew wondered. While he dressed, the question kept returning to his mind.

Shortly before four o'clock, Mathew, shining and pressed, but mystified, walked through the new-fallen snow to call on Lafayette. The city streets, so deeply rutted and littered with offal from the markets, were transformed before his eyes by the sifting blanket of white. The small, grubby houses of the poor, huddled together around the wharves, looked as bright and clean under the cover of snow as did the fine brick of the State House and the homes of the wealthy that stretched to

the west and south. The noises of the city were hushed, and men and women seemed unreal and ghostlike as they glided through the streets. For the last month, it seemed to Mathew, he had been in a trance. Once more he felt alive.

He found the Marquis de Lafayette the same charming gentleman he remembered. "My friend," Lafayette said as he clasped Mathew's hand, "it is good to see you once again. We do meet in widely separated places." In response to Mathew's questioning look, he laughed and continued, "Ah, yes, I see you are curious how I knew where to find you. I met your friend, Mr. Wallace, at Mount Vernon. As you no doubt know, he is teaching in Virginia. You, I hear, are still being persecuted." With a gesture, he invited his guest to be seated.

"My pen always seems to get me into trouble," said Mathew, sinking into a big chair. "I can't suppress my honest opinions," he added.

"Don't ever try, my friend. We need men who are willing to stand up for their convictions," answered the Marquis.

"True, sir," Mathew replied, "but it would be nice if only occasionally the ideas of those in authority agreed with mine."

Lafayette laughed heartily, then asked, "What do you propose to do here in America?"

"For the present, I must look for work," answered Mathew, and added, "As soon as I get funds from home, I hope to establish a newspaper."

"By all means, my friend, start a newspaper," the Marquis urged. "The free exchange of ideas will keep this new country strong."

The two men chatted for several minutes about Philadelphia until a servant announced other callers. Shortly after, Mathew rose and took his leave, saying, "I thank you, sir. You have done much to hearten a lone soul."

As he left the London Coffee House to return to his lodgings, Mathew noticed that the snow had stopped and a pale December sun set the whole world glistening. Every crunching step he took gave him new courage. He determined to find work the following day, rather than wait until he had enough money to start his paper.

The next morning before breakfast, Mr. Sutter handed Mathew another note, which he took to his room to avoid the curious glances of his fellow boarders. He broke the seal, and when he unfolded the letter, some bills fluttered to the floor. Mathew ignored them while he read:

Dear Mr. Carey,

. . . Your enterprise interests me very much. This wonderful new country needs a means of expressing opinion, and you have proved that you are not too timid to hold the unpopular side. I hope you will soon find time to accomplish your dream.

LAFAYETTE

Only after he read the message did Mathew stoop to retrieve the money: four one-hundred- dollar notes drawn on the Bank of North America. Lafayette had made no reference to the money enclosed.

Mathew folded the bills in the note, pocketed them, then hurriedly muffled himself against the cold and walked through the snow to the London Coffee House. He must at once thank his benefactor. But on his arrival at the inn, the host told him that the Marquis had set out for Princeton only an hour before.

Mathew returned to his lodgings at a leisurely pace. Several snowballs thrown by a group of apprentices barely missed his hat. He scooped up a handful of snow and tossed it at the boys with better aim than theirs. For the first time since he had arrived in America, he laughed out loud.

With money now in his pocket, Mathew Carey set out to make his dream of a newspaper a reality. He stopped at the St. George and the Dragon to ask his friend, the host, where he could buy a printing press.

"There are none manufactured here," the innkeeper told him. "Unless you buy one secondhand, you'll have to import it from Europe."

Why not a secondhand press? Mathew thought. With a small outlay of his capital, he could begin to publish a paper at once.

All that morning, he went from one printer to another to inquire if there were a press for sale. He could find none, and at dinnertime returned to his lodgings on Water Street, tired and discouraged. How could he disappoint Lafayette because he lacked equipment?

His problems uppermost in his mind, Mathew began to eat without a word. One of the boarders who noticed that Mathew was downcast asked why he had such a long face.

"I've been looking for a printing press, but it seems there is not one to be had," answered Mathew as he helped himself generously to potatoes.

"What about Bell's press?" the boarder volunteered. "He died last month and I hear that the heirs are to put his shop up at auction."

Mathew leaped to his feet. "Where is this shop, where . . ."

"Now, Mr. Carey," said his landlady kindly, "do sit down and finish your meal. The press will wait, I'm sure, until you've had your tea."

Mathew smiled at Mrs. Sutter, who reminded him of his

mother. He finished his dinner, then took time to write to Lafayette to thank him for his generosity. He added that although he could not accept such a sum as a gift, he was happy to accept it as a loan to be paid at a future date.

After posting his letter, Mathew went to Bell's shop to examine the press. He found that although old, it could be put in workable condition. If he could buy it cheaply, he would have more capital left to run the paper.

Certain that his problems were solved, he prepared an advertisement that announced the establishment of a press supporting the Constitutionalists, the first issue to appear on the twenty-fifth of January. Mathew's days suddenly became full, and his energy increased.

Within a week, he received a third note from the Marquis. Mr. Sutter, driven by curiosity, handed it to him at mealtime, with an acid remark. The other boarders watched while Mathew glanced at the address and put the message in his pocket, then finished his dinner as though he himself were not burning to know its contents.

As soon as he could escape to his room, he opened the letter. Lafayette had written that the important thing was to establish the newspaper. He would follow Monsieur Carey's progress from France. The money, he added, could be discussed later. Mathew was gratified to think that he had already committed himself to publishing his paper.

Impatiently, he awaited the day of the auction of Bell's shop. Bidding on the goods was slack. Books that Mr. Bell had in stock sold for a few dollars.

Mathew bought some office furniture and cases of type for very little. At last the auctioneer put the press on the block.

Mathew stood up. "I'll bid ten dollars," he said.

"Fifteen," came from the rear of the room.

"Twenty," bid Mathew.

"Twenty-five," came the same voice.

Mathew strained to catch a glimpse of his opponent. "Who is that bidder?" he inquired of the man next to him.

"Colonel Oswald of the *Independent Gazette*," the man volunteered. "Wonder why he wants that piece of worn-out machinery. He brought over presses from Europe not five years ago."

It became clear to Mathew why his opponent was bidding. He knew that Colonel Oswald was the publisher of a violently Republican paper. If he intended to stifle competition, he would find out he could not frighten a Carey so easily. Mathew set his jaw. Somehow an issue of the *Pennsylvania Evening Herald* must appear on January 25, 1785. Mathew Carey had given his word. No matter what the cost, he must have that press!

"Fifty dollars!" he shouted.

The heated bidding continued, much to the amusement of the bystanders. Finally, the press was knocked down to Mathew Carey for one hundred and fifty dollars, the price of a new one.

Even though one-third of his money was gone, Mathew was satisfied, for true to his word, he published the first issue on time. It looked good to him as it came off the press. He mailed copies to his few subscribers, then gave bundles of the papers to newsboys. He then closed the shop and walked down High Street to the accompaniment of boys calling;

"Read all about it! Get your *Pennsylvania Evening Herald*. Just off the press!"

Their raucous voices came triumphantly to his ears. At last

he had begun his career in America. He was gratified to see the number of men who stopped the boys to buy papers.

The newspaper was well received. Each issue called for a larger edition. The Newly Adopted Sons of the United States, a society of recent immigrants, found that the newspaper expressed their views and supported it, as did many others.

After a few months, Mathew found it necessary to take in two partners. Together they struggled to keep the paper alive on a small amount of capital. One day, Mathew opened the mail, which consisted mostly of bills. He paused to reread one message, then called to his partners to come see the letter he waved at them. Mr. Spottswood, one of the partners, took the letter and read:

> *Sir,*
>
> *I purposed as soon as I understood you intended to become the publisher of a newspaper in Philadelphia, to request that a copy of your product might be sent to me. I was more pleased with the determination when by a letter from my friend the Marquis de Lafayette, I found he has interested himself in your behalf . . .*
>
> *G. WASHINGTON*

The young publisher was heartened to know that his efforts had the endorsement of so great a man. But General Washington was only one of many who interested themselves in the young Irishman. Before long, he had met many prominent Philadelphians. Through letters of introduction sent him by Benjamin Franklin and the Marquis de Lafayette, Mathew soon was invited to join the literary societies and take part in the social life of the city.

Among the young ladies he met was a Miss Boys. She was lovely, charming, but haughty. Before long, Mathew Carey fell in love with the belle. But when he asked her father if he might marry her, Mr. Boys flew into a rage.

"How dare you, a poor Irish immigrant, be so impertinent as to think you are good enough for my daughter?" he ranted.

Without another word, Mathew picked up his hat and walked out of the house. He determined to devote his time only to business in the future, until he could afford a wife.

True to his resolution, Mathew gave up his social life all that summer. He spent many hours at the State House where the Assembly was meeting. Since he had the ability to remember word for word what he heard or read, he found it easy to listen to speeches and reprint them in the paper exactly as they were delivered in Assembly. Partly because of this unique reporting, the *Pennsylvania Evening Herald* soon became one of the country's leading newspapers.

Although the paper had a wide circulation, it ran into money difficulties. Carey's capital was so meager that he was constantly distressed about meeting bills. In addition, he was harried by Colonel Oswald of the *Independent Gazette* who tried every trick to cause him to fail.

One evening in November, 1785, Mathew Carey was walking down High Street as dusk was settling over the city. Mingled with other street cries, he heard boys hawking the issue of Colonel Oswald's paper, the *Independent Gazette,* that was just off the press.

A servant had set lamps in the windows of the Indian Queen Inn, and Mathew paused in their light to speak to a friend who was striding toward him. Mr. Robert Rainey, an ardent member of the Newly Adopted Sons of the United States, and an Irishman with a temperament like Mathew's, had become a close friend of the young editor. Tonight,

Mathew saw anger in his face.

While still a few feet away, he waved a folded newspaper toward Mathew, saying, "Now he calls us 'Foreign renegades'!"

Mathew took the paper from his friend and glanced at the lead article. Mr. Rainey leaned over Mathew's shoulder to point a shaking finger at a paragraph.

Mathew read aloud, "'No office of honor, trust, or profit in the United States for any person of foreign birth.'"

As he read on, Mathew's face turned waxy. He recalled his youth and the long years spent under the galling Penal Laws. The same tragic situation must not arise in America.

"Answer him, Mathew. Don't let him go unchallenged," urged his outraged friend.

Calmly, Mathew folded the *Independent Gazette* and returned it to Robert Rainey. "My paper will fight Colonel Oswald with every trick at its command," he said.

Two days later, the *Pennsylvania Evening Herald* began its war of words. The language Carey used was as vehement as that employed by Oswald.

Mr. Spottswood read the article with disapproval and commented, "This spells trouble for us."

"My words are no more violent than his, sir," replied Mathew heatedly. "Would you have us cringe before the scoundrel?"

The feud continued so long that Mathew, weary of the skirmishes, published a poem in pamphlet form, in which he accused the colonel of cowardly and unwarranted attacks on the new citizens of America.

The response was prompt. The day after the pamphlet went on sale, a friend of Oswald's called at the office of the *Pennsylvania Evening Herald*.

"Captain Rice, at your service, sir," said the man, making

a stiff bow. "Colonel Oswald instructed me to tell you that he considers this a challenge," he added as he placed a copy of Mathew's pamphlet on the desk.

The editor bowed slightly in return, picked up his pamphlet, and answered coolly, "It was so intended, sir."

Mathew then named a French merchant, Mr. Marmie, as his second, and assured Captain Rice his friend would call to make arrangements for the duel. The captain bowed once more and his back rigid as though on parade, he left the shop.

Fascinated by the captain's military bearing, the young publisher stepped to the window to watch him stride down the street.

"The colonel will make short work of me," he said over his shoulder to his partner. "I don't even know how to handle a pistol."

Then Mathew picked up his hat and went to tell Mr. Marmie of the duty thrust upon him.

His friend protested, "A duel is no solution at all."

Mathew smiled faintly and said, "I agree with you, but I am honor-bound to carry it out."

Unable to dissuade the young publisher, Mr. Marmie agreed to act as his second.

While he walked to his lodgings, Mathew pondered on the strange paradox that his first trouble came about because he wrote about a duel, and now he was forced to fight a duel because of what he had written. He still was opposed to dueling, but felt in this instance there was no other solution.

Word of the duel spread and became a general topic of conversation. Mathew took the whole matter calmly, but said to his partner, "My greatest fear is that I should tremble and give the impression of cowardice."

Just before dawn on Wednesday, which was the day arranged for the affair, Mathew and his second stood on the banks of the Delaware, watching the ferry break the thin rim of ice as it nosed into shore. No sooner were they aboard, than the ferryman pushed off for the New Jersey side.

Mathew wrapped his cloak around himself a little tighter and wondered why men chose the hour of sunrise, the most awe-inspiring time of day, on which to destroy one another. It was part of the imbecility of the whole business, but it was too late now to seek another remedy. He shrugged and turned to speak to his friend who seemed sunk in despair.

"Cheer up," he said, "I feel as cool as though I were paying a social call instead of risking death because of a few hasty words."

"Why did you refuse to let me give you a few lessons in the use of the pistol?" asked Mr. Marmie, clutching the case of firearms, and looking fearfully at the approaching shore.

"Because I object to handling firearms if I don't have to. I do not intend to aim at the colonel," answered Mathew casually.

"I only hope he feels the same way!" replied his friend.

The boat scraped the Jersey bank, and the ferryman jumped out to tie the small craft to a tree. The two friends left the boat and hurried to the appointed meeting place. They found Colonel Oswald, Captain Rice, and a doctor— shadowy, unreal figures, grouped together a few feet from the ferry landing. Dawn was about to break. The barren trees loomed dark against the slaty sky.

Captain Rice came forward to meet Mr. Marmie to make final arrangements. Mathew took off his cloak, folded it methodically, put it on a tree stump, and placed his hat on top. He then turned to receive his instructions.

The affair of honor took only a few minutes. Mathew did exactly as he was told. He paced off the required number of steps, turned, and at the signal, fired in the air. At the same moment he heard the colonel's shot and felt a sting in his leg. Slowly he sank to the ground. Captain Rice helped Maurice Marmie carry the victim to the boat.

Now that Colonel Oswald had proved his courage by fighting the duel, Mathew felt honor-bound to withdraw his charges of cowardice. When shortly after his recovery, he met his friends for dinner, Mathew announced his intention of making a retraction. Immediately, a babble of voices arose. His friends demanded to know if he intended to make a public apology.

Mathew ate his dinner with relish and ignored the hornets' nest he had brought about his ears.

"If you're turning into a bootlicker, we'll have naught to do with you," flared Robert Rainey as he pushed his chair back so violently that it overturned.

His other friends rose, too, color high in their faces.

"I'm merely doing the man a simple justice," Mathew told them as he looked from one to another.

Without a word, the friends whom he had defended turned and left. Mathew watched them go, then called for pen and paper to compose his apology. He took it to the office to meet the deadline for the next issue of the paper. With this gesture, the feud died.

7

NEW VENTURES

MATHEW CAREY had been in Philadelphia for almost a year before Benjamin Franklin returned from France. Along with most of the other citizens, he went to the dock to greet the great man, but could only catch a glimpse of his friend through the dense crowd. He thought it only fair to give the old man a few days rest before he called on him. In the meantime, however, Franklin's grandson stopped in the newspaper office to say that he brought word from Dr. Franklin that Mathew was to come to supper the following evening.

Precisely at six, Mathew let fall the knocker on the Franklin door. The maid showed him into the drawing room where Franklin stood by the window talking to some men. As soon as he saw Carey, he came forward with extended hand.

"Mathew, how good of you to come," he said, and before the young man could reply, introduced him to the assembled guests, saying here was a young firebrand with a passion for defending a cause—that he and Mathew Carey had the same goal of peace, but Carey insisting on attaining his ends by means of a good fight.

To Mathew, Dr. Franklin looked much the same as he had in Passy. He was a little portlier perhaps, his thinning hair grayer, but he had the same keen glance and friendly smile.

From the first reunion, the old man and his young friend delighted in the company of one another, enjoying each other's wit and laughing at the same jokes. Franklin introduced Mathew Carey to the members of the American Philosophical Society. The meetings were held in Franklin's home, and there Mathew met such famous men as Thomas Jefferson and Alexander Hamilton, proud to be accepted among the learned and distinguished men of the city.

In the business field, however, the young Irishman was becoming restless. Although he had owned the newspaper for little over a year, he found it offered no challenge now that Colonel Oswald had ceased to badger him, and opposition to the idea of a Constitution was weakening. Often his thoughts turned to the impossibility of Americans finding a publisher for their writings. Some of the essays, stories, and poems sent to his paper were every bit as good as those included in books from England, yet, since the newspapers had a small circulation, few would ever read these fine pieces.

To help remedy the situation, Mathew thought of publishing a magazine to reprint essays that had appeared here and there in newspapers throughout the country. One day he broached the subject to Franklin who approved of the idea and suggested that Mathew interest the Philosophical Society in the periodical.

"I'll bring the matter up at the meeting next Friday night," said Franklin.

That Friday, Mathew arrived early for the meeting. He always enjoyed the papers read, but this time Mathew thought them both long and dull. The others, however, seemed to be listening with the usual attention and interest. Following the formal meeting, the group sat down to the regular supper of oysters and beer. The young man glanced at Franklin who gave no sign that he remembered about the magazine. Could it be that his memory was failing? Had he forgotten? Deep in thought,

Mathew lost the thread of conversation. He came to with a start when he heard Franklin turn the conversation to literature.

He was saying, "No country can be great if it lacks a literature of its own."

The British, he added, thought Americans were barbarians, and local printers were too cowardly to risk losing money on books by a fellow citizen. Except for a sermon or two and some moral tracts, scarcely any books by Americans were being published. The old man glanced over at Mathew as though to say, Son, here is your opportunity. Make the most of it.

Delighted at the opening, Mathew leaned forward to say that he had in mind a way to remedy the situation. Then he explained in detail his plan for a reprint magazine while the members of the Philosophical Society listened intently. Between Franklin's questions and Mathew's enthusiasm, they convinced the Society of the wisdom of such an undertaking. Through their endorsement, Mathew succeeded in finding two partners to help publish the magazine that he called the *American Museum*.

Mr. Spottswood, his newspaper partner, had refused to join in the new venture. He said, "Carey, I can't understand you. You are still in debt for the newspaper. You have no right to begin a magazine. Since you have neither capital for such an enterprise nor equipment to print a magazine, you are bound to fail and I want no part of such nonsense."

Not in the least discouraged by Mr. Spottswood's prediction of calamity, Mathew began to gather the best material he could find, for he intended his periodical to be of the highest quality.

Though his leg pained him and he was in poor health, he, himself, set the type for most of the first issue. The edition of one thousand copies was published in January, 1787, and was promptly sold out. Too optimistic about the demand for the magazine, the owners overprinted the succeeding issues and lost money.

Unfortunately for the venture, cash was very scarce in the year 1787. Many who had subscribed had difficulty in making payments. Mathew, on checking his accounts, found most of the overdue subscriptions to be in outlying districts.

"Someone will have to collect these bills," he said, "and also search out new subscribers."

It was agreed that Mathew should make a journey through the countryside. He looked forward to the trip, for although he had spent almost three years in the city of Philadelphia, his knowledge of other parts of America was only hearsay. At last he was to have an opportunity to see some of the country for himself. Without delay, he bought a horse and began his expedition.

Not knowing what to expect, Mathew rode up the stagecoach road toward Reading. The country was sparsely settled. Between forests of great oaks and chestnuts, he came to patches of tilled land. The fields he passed were yellow with ripening wheat, with blue cornflowers and wild roses blooming on their borders.

His first call was at a farmhouse. The housewife, although delighted to sit for an hour and listen to Mathew talk of the magazine, told him regretfully that her family could not subscribe. Since everyone rose at dawn and worked through the heat of the day, all were abed shortly after sunset. Winter was scarcely better, with the care of the barns and livestock. The young ones barely had time to learn their letters, and the older folk read nothing but the paper. They did not even own a Bible.

When the young man was rested and refreshed, the farm wife directed him to the nearest village. To his relief, Mathew found money a little more plentiful in the villages and towns. In each he met subscribers, yet for every one who could settle his bill, there were three who asked for credit. Although saddlesore and weary, he rode through New York and Pennsylvania, then down through the hills to Virginia, each day adding another thirty miles to his travels. He talked to men in all walks of life. Again and again people spoke of not being able to buy a Bible within their means.

Mathew Carey made note of everything he saw and heard, especially about the Bible, yet his immediate concern was the *American Museum*. Although the magazine was losing money, its publisher was confident that since the country needed such a magazine so badly, the venture would survive.

Mathew returned from his trip so fired up with enthusiasm, that he would have liked to devote more time to the magazine. Events in Philadelphia, though, forced him to give most of his attention to the *Pennsylvania Evening Herald*.

The State Assembly was debating its course of action should the Constitution be adopted by Congress, and Mathew had to spend many hours at the State House, reporting speeches for the newspaper.

At last, to his gratification, the delegates to the Convention signed the Constitution on September 7, 1787, and referred it to the states.

In every issue of the paper, Mathew explained, cajoled, and demanded that Pennsylvania accept the Constitution. He wrote that their own Benjamin Franklin had urged its passage, saying that while no one liked all the provisions, it was in general good. On December 12, Carey was present when the votes were recorded. At last Pennsylvania had ratified the Constitution, and he joined in the shouts of jubilation.

Spontaneously, the spectators paraded down Chestnut Street. Men flocked from every home to join in, waving flags and shouting. Excitement ran high, and Mathew Carey was in the midst of it.

Tired, but elated, he returned that night to the printing office and announced to his partners that with the ratification of the Constitution, the work of the *Pennsylvania Evening Herald* was completed. "I will now withdraw from the partnership and sell my share of the newspaper," he said.

This was done the following February, and now that he had only the *American Museum* to occupy him, Mathew felt he dare indulge in his dream of two years. He would start on his most ambitious undertaking: to publish the Bible.

One Saturday afternoon when he made his customary call on Franklin, Mathew Carey mentioned his desire to print both the Douay and King James versions of the Bible so that it might be read both by Catholics and Protestants. Franklin smiled. "And how do you propose to go about the gigantic business of publishing the Scriptures, my impetuous friend?" he asked.

"There must be a way, the need is so great," Mathew replied thoughtfully.

"If you plan such a project," Franklin said, "you must consult about the Douay version with the Vicar-General of the Catholic Church in the United States: my good friend, John Carroll, who will soon be your first bishop."

Mathew said that he had written to Father Carroll about his idea and had received a most enthusiastic reply, but now that he was giving serious thought to the work, he agreed it was time to go consult with the Vicar-General in person.

Shortly thereafter, Mathew took a packet to Baltimore, and he immediately went to call on Father Carroll. The kindly priest received him graciously. When they were comfortably settled, he said, "Mr. Carey, I have wanted to tell you personally of the importance I attach to the *American Museum*."

"Thank you, Father Carroll," replied Mathew, "but I came to Baltimore to consult with you on the advisability of publishing the Bible."

"There is no doubt," said the priest, leaning forward in his chair, "that such a work is a dire necessity in this country. In fact, the Douay version of the Bible is out-of-print in England also." Then he glanced at Mathew's modest clothing and added, "It will be a very expensive work. Can you afford to undertake such a venture?"

"Frankly, no," answered Mathew, "but if it must be done, I see no reason why I shouldn't be the one to do it."

The Vicar-General smiled and offered to help by securing as many subscriptions as possible, saying that as soon as the list was opened, he wanted his name put down for twenty copies. He said that he felt he should warn Mr. Carey that the Catholics in America were few in number and not very prosperous.

"My Bible will be within the means of everyone," declared Mathew.

With Father Carroll's blessing on his work, Mathew returned to Philadelphia. While sailing up the river, he composed a full-page advertisement for the Bible to be run on the back of the *American Museum*. On his return, he also requested the priests of the city to mention the work from the pulpit. Through inquiry, he had discovered that few of his friends owned a copy of Holy Writ, and most of the copies in existence were in deplorable condition. There was a real need even in his own city.

The pastor of St. Mary's preached that Sunday about the sacredness of the Scriptures and stated that everyone should own a copy. He said he was happy to announce that a member of their own congregation, Mathew Carey, was willing, at great financial risk to himself, to publish such a work and St. Mary's congregation should lend its support by subscribing.

When his friends flocked around him after Mass and predicted his failure, Mathew insisted that he could not see why.

"The greatest book ever given to mankind will have a market in America," he stated. "It must be printed here. I intend to publish the Bible."

Subscriptions began to trickle in. A friend dropped into the office one day and noticed the box of subscriptions on the publisher's desk.

"What do you intend to do with these?" he asked as he ruffled through them. "You haven't a line of Holy Writ in type."

"But I soon will, my friend," answered Mathew with more confidence than he felt.

Now that he was in duty bound to produce a Bible, he set to work in earnest. Determined that it would be as free from error as possible, he read and compared eighteen editions.

"How many pages will the work run," a friend asked curiously.

"Approximately a thousand," answered Mathew, and smiled at the awe in the man's eyes.

Although he had spoken with confidence, Mathew was concerned about how he could produce such a mammoth work. With patience he could edit the Bible, but he did not own type that was good enough to print Holy Scripture. His problem was solved by a newspaper advertisement that John Baine and Company, formerly of Edinburgh, Scotland, intended to establish a type foundry in Philadelphia.

Immediately, he called on Mr. Baine, and found him in his shirtsleeves as he directed the placement of his machinery. Mathew sat on a keg while he spoke to the busy man of his plan for publishing the Bible.

"I'll be happy to give you a good price on my best type for such a fine purpose," said the type founder, pausing to talk business.

True to his word, Mr. Baine supplied Mathew Carey with enough new finely cut type to set up both the Douay and the King James versions of the Scriptures, and made liberal terms for payment.

On November 14, 1789, Mathew had the satisfaction of seeing the first page of his Bible come off the press. The printer handed him the sheet as he drew it off. The publisher examined it critically.

"In the beginning," he read, "God created the heaven and the earth . . ." The type stood out, bold and clear, on the good white page.

Mathew was silent as he envisioned Carey Bibles in home after home all over the land. The foreman of the print shop broke into his reverie. "How many copies are to be printed before we break up the type?" he asked.

Mathew stood for a long moment as he looked at the forms, then turned to the printer and said gravely. "This type, as you know, was cast especially for the Bible. I intend to keep it set up for as long as I need to print Bibles, and that will be as long as I am in business."

8

BRIDGET

IN JANUARY, 1790, Mathew discussed his affairs with his friend, Benjamin Franklin.

"How is it possible," he asked, "that I could have reached my thirtieth year and still be in financial difficulties, while others younger than I have made their fortunes?"

Franklin looked over the top of his glasses at the man sitting across from him and asked, "Would you be content to give up your ideas and be a merchant all your life?"

The old man settled himself more comfortably and pulled the shawl closely around his shoulders, then added in his quavering voice, "Put your ideas into action, Mathew, and don't worry about making money."

For some months Franklin's health had been failing, and Mathew feared to tire him. He was about ready to leave when Franklin's daughter signaled from the door and Mathew rose, looking sadly at his friend whose head nodded almost before he had ceased to speak. But, before Mathew had left the room, the old man roused himself to say, "God bless you, my boy."

"And you, too, sir," answered Mathew, who turned away sadly, knowing his friend would not live much longer.

Benjamin Franklin died on April 7, 1790. Mathew felt he had lost a second father. Over twenty thousand attended the funeral. The professors and students of the University of Pennsylvania came in a body, as did the members of the fire company, the library, and the various societies that he had founded.

As Mathew walked in the cortege with the members of the American Philosophical Society, he recalled the statesman's many kindnesses to him when he was an exiled boy in France, and the warm friendship Franklin had shared with him the five years Mathew had lived in Philadelphia.

As a tribute to the great man, in July, 1790, the *American Museum* carried the first section of the *Autobiography of Benjamin Franklin*.

His thirtieth year was not all sadness for Mathew Carey however. He spent many enjoyable evenings, for a bachelor was a welcome guest at parties throughout the city. Even though his fortune was not yet made, his resolution to remain single faded, for once more Mathew fell in love, this time with a young lady by the name of Bridget Flahavan who was ten years his junior. Mathew was captivated by her lighthearted laughter and the mischief in her bright blue eyes. He thought the dark curls at the nape of her neck enchanting. She was gentle yet merry-hearted.

One evening at a dance, she came toward him, saying that she would just have to rest awhile. Since he had watched her many times as she danced through the whole evening, he realized that she wanted to sit with him and was flattered. He was delighted by her merry chatter, but did not dare hope she was interested in him.

As they sat watching a minuet, he said, "Miss Bridget, I would give a great deal to have the honor to lead a dance with you on my arm."

He was gratified to see how prettily she blushed as she told him she was most content to watch.

Soon he became a constant visitor at the Flahavan home. After a glorious summer of picnics and music in the company of Bridget, Mathew spoke to her father about his love for the young lady, and at the same time explained his fears about seeking her hand.

Mr. Flahavan said he was sure the difference in their ages would not be important to Bridget if she were in love with Mathew, which he thought quite likely. But, Mr. Flahavan added in all fairness, he must mention his impoverished condition, because he had no dowry to give his daughter. Mathew hastened to assure his prospective father-in-law that money was not even to be considered.

Mathew found it much easier to speak to her father than to Bridget. Suppose she would laugh at him and say he was old and lame? But then he berated himself for such ideas, for no one as kind and gentle as Bridget would say such things, but he dreaded reading rejection in her candid eyes. The thought that she might send him away was almost unbearable, yet he must know if he could hope.

After all his worry about a fitting time and place to propose, he chanced to find Bridget alone in her parlor one day and blurted out that he loved her.

"I love you too, Mathew," she answered shyly.

Then, without his quite knowing how, he was holding her in his arms, murmuring, "Bridget, my darling."

After a moment he drew away and said, "You must know, my dear, that although I love you dearly, I am a poor man and cannot give you the luxuries you deserve."

"Mathew," she replied indignantly, "it's you I love, not your money. Don't you realize that?"

"Forgive me, dear," answered Mathew. "It is just that I want the best for you."

The couple planned to be married in February. Mathew found a house on High Street near Fourth that Bridget thought beautiful. Long hours were spent in discussion of the future. Mathew found his fiancee interested and encouraging when he spoke of business affairs. Especially did she listen carefully as he told her about his problems in publishing the Bible.

On the first of December, 1790, the first printing of his Bible was completed. Mathew ordered the first copy especially bound in fine Morocco. Then with the bulky bundle under his arm, he hurried to the Flahavan home. Bridget greeted him at the door, and he thrust his package into her hands, saying: "This, my love, is for you."

She untied the string and took from its wrapping a handsomely bound volume of the Holy Bible.

"Oh, Mathew, it is finished at last!" she exclaimed. "How beautiful!"

Mathew looked over her shoulder as she examined the soft leather binding and the clean, clearly printed pages.

"See, Bridget," he said as he opened the volume, "here is a page for our family record."

The first item to go into the Carey family page was the marriage of Mathew Carey to Bridget Flahavan on Thursday, the 24th of February, 1791. The wedding was simple. Following the mode of the day, the groom wore his hair cropped, glad to be rid of the queue. His bride was lovely in her Sunday dress and a new blue bonnet with roses beneath the brim.

Only Bridget's family was present at St. Mary's to hear the couple make their vows. After the ceremony, they all returned to the Flahavans for refreshments. Amidst much laughter and teasing, everyone drank the bride's health in strong tea.

Mathew thought they'd never have enough. He had placed his spoon across his cup a good twenty minutes before the others finished, and Bridget, blushing prettily, rose to say they had better be going before it got too dark. All crowded around to bid Bridget good-bye while her mother shed a tear or two.

The cart with Mathew's furniture stopped before the house. Willing hands helped pile Bridget's feather bed and chest upon it, and it started off slowly for the new house. Then Bridget's nephew unhitched Mathew's horse and backed the gig to the door. Mathew helped his bride into the gig and climbed in after her. He took up the reins, nodded to the boy to release the horse, and the Careys were off to their home. Lovingly, Mathew looked down at his bride who tucked her hand in his under the lap robe and turned to him with a contented sigh.

It was only a short ride to their new home, a four-story brick house with a marble cornice. Mathew had unlocked the door and carried his bride across the threshold before the slower-moving cart with their household goods clattered over the cobbles and came to a halt.

Quickly he lit a fire in each of the three downstairs rooms, while Bridget exclaimed at his extravagance. Then he untied his bride's bonnet and kissed her before he took it off.

But they had no time to waste, for the carter had carried in their possessions and Mathew and Bridget bustled around to help him place the furniture before the light failed. When all the furniture was in place, Mathew looked about his home.

How much they lacked! Should he not even have gone into debt to provide a better setting for the beautiful wife who would keep him company here?

When Bridget came back from the kitchen, he spoke these thoughts aloud. But Bridget said, "These will do well enough until we can afford better, my dear. I'm content to wait until we have money to pay for what we want."

Mathew was blessed in such a patient wife, for business was not too profitable. The Careys depended to a great extent for their livelihood on the proceeds from the *American Museum*, for as yet not enough copies of the Bible had been sold to cover the great expense of producing it. While never a great financial success, the magazine weathered many a storm, until at last, it was sunk indirectly by a government bill.

In 1792, postal rates were set for the United States, but there was no specific rate for magazines; the fee was left to the discretion of the local postmaster. Philadelphia's postmaster was a rival printer by the name of Bradford, and he set the fee for the *American Museum* at the rate for letters. Since he could not pay the extremely high rate, Mathew Carey was forced to announce that the magazine would be discontinued.

In the evening, after making the announcement, he and Bridget sat in their front room and discussed their problems. What would Mathew do in the future?

"Whatever you want to do, my dear," she said, "I know will be right."

How can I possibly live up to such faith in me? thought Mathew. He looked at Bridget and recalled the ambitions of his youth. "All my life I've wanted to be a publisher and seller of books," he said.

"Then, that you shall be," she told him. "Your Bible is beautiful. If you can publish that great work, you can do the same for others."

Bridget looked around her prized front drawing room and said that she had no need of two rooms in which to sit. This parlor would do very well as a bookstore when lined with shelves. With his wife's faith in him and the sacrifice of her treasured room, Mathew knew he dare not fail. He gathered together his small stock of books, the greater number being Bibles and spelling books, and opened a store in his home.

The store prospered, for times were good and money plentiful. Bridget and Mathew were happy, for now they had a baby girl. To her parents there was no infant in Philadelphia as smart and beautiful as their Maria.

As time wore on, Mathew became more concerned about the fate of the immigrants from all countries. Since so many of them were city dwellers and factory workers, they found very little employment for their skills in agricultural America. Many of the Irish, having either known or heard of Carey, gravitated to his shop.

One afternoon Bridget looked up from the cradle, where she had placed Maria, to find Mathew standing in the doorway. He was flanked by two Irish lads with coats too small and neat patches on their breeches. In their big, work-worn hands each held a pitifully small bundle.

"Come in," she said. "Tread softly, for the baby is asleep."

"These lads," said Mathew, "come with a letter from my mother. I thought they might like a dish of tea before I take them to the print shop."

Mrs. Carey graciously served tea to the awe-stricken boys and smiled at their obvious dread of dropping the china.

That evening after dinner she protested mildly, "Mathew, you can't take care of all the Irish who apply to you."

"I know, my dear. The shop is bursting with them now, and I not knowing where I'll get the wherewithal to pay their wages."

He cupped his chin in his hands for a moment, then continued thoughtfully, "But I have invited some of our friends to discuss the matter with me."

Mathew and his friends formed a Hibernian Society that helped many Irish immigrants to keep their families together while they were establishing themselves in the new country.

The contentment of the Careys was disturbed in the summer of 1793 by the appalling yellow fever epidemic that swept the city. Many fled, but Mathew Carey refused to go, saying he might be needed, and Bridget would not leave without him.

In desperation, the Mayor called a citizens meeting early in September.

"I must go; I'm sure I can be of some service," said Mathew to his wife. He picked up his hat and bent to kiss Bridget who watched him anxiously as he left the house.

He walked up High Street and turned down Fifth Street toward City Hall. As he neared the building he saw only one man entering it ahead of him. Could he be late? At the door of the Assembly room he paused in astonishment. The Mayor sat alone on the raised platform that was usually crowded with dignitaries. Only a handful of men were scattered throughout the hall.

At last the Mayor rose and spoke to the few present. He outlined the problems presented by the disaster and asked that a committee be formed to take on the responsibility of the city in the crisis. Mathew Carey and a dozen others agreed to serve. For six weeks he devoted all of his time to the sufferers, and gradually order was brought out of chaos.

During the course of the fever, Mathew and another member of the committee had to drive out to the dread contagious hospital on business. They had no intention of going any closer than necessary, but they chanced to meet the doctor at the gate. He greeted them affably and invited them to inspect the hospital.

His friend refused, but Mathew hopped from the carriage and followed the doctor into the hospital. He toured the building and spoke to the sick. No visitor had ever been seen in the hospital, and the patients were astounded at a well man walking amongst them.

When he returned to the carriage, his companion drew himself as far away as he could, saying, "Why did you unnecessarily expose yourself and us to the plague? I can't understand such foolishness."

"Neither can I," Mathew replied, smiling briefly as he picked up the reins. "But I have more sympathy for those poor people since I have seen them in their distress."

When he reached home, he spoke of the incident lightly, not wishing to alarm his wife. "How could I refuse the doctor?" he asked. "He is only a man like myself, yet he exposes himself to illness constantly. I will not act the coward."

"You could never do that," replied Bridget and brushed her hand gently across his forehead, testing for fever. For Mathew's sake, she pretended to take the visit lightly, but in her heart was sure that her husband would contract the disease.

That night, Mathew, too, went to bed convinced he had caught the fever, but the next morning rose laughing at his fears. He had escaped the plague.

By the end of October, the yellow fever abated. Citizens on

their return to the city found many of their friends missing. Whole families were wiped out, businesses ruined, and many unemployed. Mathew Carey was delegated to write an account of the disaster. Since he helped care for the poor, the ill, and the orphaned, he was well qualified. To his careful account he added a list of the dead, which he secured through a door-to-door census.

Finally, December 12 was proclaimed a day of Thanksgiving for deliverance from the plague. Church bells rang, and the people hastened to give thanks to God.

Three days later, the Careys had another reason to rejoice, for their first son Henry was born. The year 1793 was truly a memorable one, with death and devastation followed by calm and happiness.

9

PARSON WEEMS

AFTER the yellow fever epidemic, the demand for Carey books grew. Mathew found it necessary to take many trips, sometimes by horseback and sometimes by stage. He often returned from these trips ill and exhausted. Bridget insisted that he could not continue and urged him to engage help.

A solution of his problems seemed at hand one day in 1795 when the door to his shop opened and a small rotund man in clerical garb came in and introduced himself as Parson Weems. White hair flowed from under a wide-brimmed black hat with a goose-quill pen stuck jauntily in the brim. His black suit showed the dust of the road. A small inkwell suspended from his lapel jiggled with every step. The parson lost no time in announcing himself as a book agent who would like to sell the Carey books.

"Why do you want to sell books?" the publisher inquired.

With a wink and a smile, the man replied, "Good to the

public and pleasure and profit to ourselves will result from replenishing the earth with books."

Carey laughed heartily at the little parson's remark and promptly engaged him to vend the Carey books throughout the Southern states. From this beginning, Mathew soon appointed agents in other sections of the country.

Parson Weems combined selling Carey books with marrying, or burying, or christening wherever he found a need for his services. Soon the Carey name became a byword in every place he visited. He also helped Mathew in his cherished dream of encouraging writers. Even though the *American Museum* had failed, Mathew never lost sight of the purpose for which he had established the magazine. He even offered his agents greater commissions on every book by American authors that they sold.

"Whenever you find someone who has written a good book," he said to the parson, "send him to me."

Parson Weems eagerly searched out authors until finally Carey was forced to write him, "For heaven's sake, don't refer to me everyone who has put pen to paper."

The publishing business continued to expand; during the years 1792-1799, Carey did a business of $300,000. At times he employed as many as 150 printers. The Carey family was increasing, too, and soon outgrew its home. By 1800, there were three small sisters, Catherine, Eleanor, and Frances, to play with Maria. The four little girls were constantly underfoot, and, although Mathew kept Henry with him in the shop, there was simply not enough room to live in comfort.

So the Careys moved to a larger house at the corner of Fourth and Chestnut Streets, a short block from Independence

Hall. As in his old home, he converted the front rooms into a bookstore. In this way, Bridget could supervise the business when her husband was away. Mathew had another reason for keeping the business at home. Henry had become his shadow, and, although Mathew would not admit it to anyone, he felt better if the darkeyed little son were near.

Parson Weems continued to be the chief agent for Carey books, but he worked in such a helter-skelter fashion that Mathew rarely knew what route his star salesman was traveling. This proved irritating when he wanted Weems in Philadelphia to discuss important matters that came up.

Once, Mathew, as usual, was having no success in locating the parson, when suddenly, one day, the little man appeared in the doorway of the bookshop. Henry ran to throw his arms around the small rotund man. The parson took off his wide-brimmed black hat, and popped it on the little boy's head, then threw an arm around his shoulder.

His employer stared at the jolly little parson, then found voice to ask, "Where have you been? I've been trying to get in touch with you. You go wandering around this country and I never know where to find you."

"Have you no kind word for me?" asked the parson, pulling up a chair and settling in it. "And I traveling all this distance for your own good. I have the makings of a new book for you to publish."

He drew a large sheet of paper toward him and plucked the quill pen from the brim of the hat which he retrieved from Henry, then dipping the pen in the little inkwell, he wrote in large letters:

THE LIFE OF GEORGE WASHINGTON

He held the sheet up for Mathew Carey to see, then sat back to enjoy the effect on his employer. In reply to Carey's question, he told him that ever since the death of Washington, he, Mason Locke Weems, had been collecting anecdotes of the great man, and now was ready to put them in a book. It would be a moral tale for old and young. He even had a story about the boy Washington chopping down his father's cherry tree that should edify many a youth.

"Is it true?" asked Carey.

"Well—let us say it is moral," replied the parson with a wink.

While the parson was writing *The Life of George Washington*, he sold a great number of other books, but he was often slow in remitting money. Mathew, desperately in need of funds, made a trip to meet Weems at his home in Dumfries, Virginia. To reach the town, he had to go by mail coach. Travel in such a vehicle was sheer torture. Plain backless wooden benches were placed over the sacks of mail, and heavy leather curtains enclosed the carriage. Passengers sat for long hours in the sweltering semidarkness.

After days of such discomfort, Mathew's temper was not improved when he reached the meeting place only to find the parson not at home. Mrs. Weems made him as comfortable as possible, but he fumed for two days until one of the children ran to tell him that "Pappy" was coming down the lane at last.

For once, the jaunty little parson had lost his spring. He was dirty and disheveled and drove at a snail's pace. His children crowded around him, and his wife greeted him affectionately as he alighted. When he saw Mathew Carey, he raised his hand to ward off any verbal blows and said:

"Please, sir, when a person has been as close to eternity as I, he is entitled to hear only kind words."

As the little man hobbled to the porch, he explained that his horse had bolted and overturned the wagon with its heavy bookcase, pinning him under the load. His rescue had been effected by an enormous slave sent by Providence at the right moment. The man had righted the wagon and freed him. The tale finished, the parson asked his wife if she knew the date.

When she told him, Wednesday, July 2, he started up.

"John Smith is to wed Sally Goforth this day!" he exclaimed. "And I promised to tie the knot. Have you some clean linen, my dear?"

"But, sir," protested Mathew. "I've come all this distance for a business talk with you."

The parson replied that he desired that, too, but surely Mathew was not so hardhearted and unfeeling as to interfere with love. He should come to the marrying and they'd hold conversation on the way. But the parson found so many other things to talk about that they reached the gathering before Mathew could bring the conversation around to finances.

They found the guests assembled and the groom impatient. The parson greeted all cheerily and promptly performed the ceremony. Then he sent to the cart for his fiddle to play for the dancing, only to find it had been broken in his accident. Someone produced another and saved the day. Mathew sat in a corner and marveled at the energy with which the parson called the figures for the dance.

When the wedding feast was about to break up, the parson announced that he had some very moral and enjoyable books with him and urged the guests to step to his carriage to examine his wares. He made enough sales to consider his evening profitable.

As he and his employer jogged home through the moonlight, Mathew remarked unfeelingly, "I hope that since you no longer have a fiddle, you will find time to write me at greater length to explain your plans." Then he went on to tell of his serious financial situation due to delays in receiving payments for books sold by his agents.

The next morning the parson gave his employer two hundred dollars and said he would remit more often if he did not have such trouble changing the money he received on his travels into notes on good banks.

"Be sure not to get notes on those Southern banks that have no gold to back them up," cautioned his employer with a worried frown.

"I will," said the parson, solemn for once. "But business will never expand," he added, "until we have sound banks we can trust. And we need good men to run them."

Mathew, having collected some money, began the journey home the next day in good humor. As he traveled, he thought how much easier running a business would be if the country had a better banking system.

On a sunny morning in 1802, shortly after his return from Dumfries, Mathew Carey went to the garden behind the house. His wife sat there embroidering while the children played around her. Maria ran to pull up a chair for her father and sat at his feet.

"I've asked Patrick to bring the mail out here. You don't mind, my dear?" he asked.

"You know, Mathew," said Bridget, "I am only too happy to see you rest awhile."

Mathew stretched his legs and closed his eyes for a minute, then sat up at the sound of footsteps.

Looking up, he saw his porter standing in the doorway, the bundle of letters in his hand.

"Ah, Patrick, thank you," Mathew said, taking the mail from the porter.

A letter from the parson topped the pile. A number of bank notes floated to the ground when Mathew broke the seal. One rested at his wife's feet, while others were caught up by a gentle breeze. Before the notes had fluttered far, the children scrambled to catch them.

As Mrs. Carey smoothed the bills that the children dropped in her lap, she remarked, "One of these is drawn on the Bank of Pennsylvania and the others on the Bank of New

York. I suppose those banks are sound."

Her husband had not heard, however. After glancing briefly at the parson's note, he sat staring at an open letter stamped with the seal of the Governor of Pennsylvania. For a long moment he gazed down, brows raised in an attitude of surprise.

Mrs. Carey asked in alarm, "Is something wrong, dear?"

As he passed her the letter, he said, "Nothing, my love. This is an appointment as a director of the Bank of Pennsylvania."

"Do you own the bank, now, Papa?" asked Eleanor.

Mathew smiled. "No, my dear, the Governor only wants me to help him run the bank," he said. Then he quipped to his wife, "I've walked down Second Street so often, going to the bank to ask for a loan, that I imagine they think I belong there."

When he accepted his new responsibilities, Mathew took time to study all phases of the banking business, and for several years he divided his time between publishing and financial affairs. In both fields he introduced ideas that either were not popular or were advanced for the times.

Among publishers, Carey stood almost alone in the way he treated his authors. During the period when there was no copyright protection for either author or publisher, he saw that they were properly paid and soon he gained a reputation for honest dealings. He also imported books from England and, after much thought, arranged with Constable and Company, publishers of the leading British novelists, to act as his agents. His firm was the first to publish the novels of Sir Walter Scott, and later of Charles Dickens, in America.

Mathew made sure that young Henry understood a publisher's responsibility to authors. He liked to have his son by his side as he drew up a contract for a new book and would introduce him to the writer.

"Remember," he said one day, "authors keep us in business. Always treat them with the honesty and respect that is their due."

Henry, who was now twelve, had announced one day that he was leaving school. Surprisingly, his father allowed him to do so. Now Henry spent many hours in the store each day, and it was not long before his father depended on him in many ways. One morning as the porter came in the door with rags and polish in his hand, having rubbed the brass name plate until it shone, Mathew looked with affection at his son and remarked, "In a few years, Henry, we'll need a new plate to read, CAREY AND SON—PUBLISHERS AND BOOKSELLERS. You are a great help to me."

The boy threw out his chest, and with face flushed, said, "Thank you, Father. Then you don't really mind my leaving school?"

"No, son, I don't mind at all, although at first I thought twelve was a bit young. You can learn much from your own reading, as I did when a boy, and from working along with me. Already you have a good head for business, and I feel you can handle almost any problem that might arise. In fact, I have decided to send you to Baltimore for a while as superintendent of the branch store."

Henry stared at his father, too astonished to speak. Finally, when he found his voice, all he could say was, "I—I'll try my best to do a good job, and not fail you."

"I have no fears on that score," replied Mathew kindly, placing his arm around the boy's shoulders.

"We'll make arrangements for you to take on your new

duties right away. Now let's go discuss it with your mother."

After Henry left for Baltimore, Mathew turned his attention to a less pleasant problem, that of Parson Weems. The agent continued so erratic in his business dealings that again his employer became exasperated. Feeling that he could no longer conduct a business in such turmoil and uncertainty, Mathew discharged his Southern agent. One consequence was that Parson Weems took his *Life of George Washington* to another publisher.

During the next two years, Mathew sorely missed the little man and his unpredictable ways. Besides, he felt the loss of the business the parson brought. One blustery March day, Mathew turned the corner of Second and Market Streets, head bowed against the wind, and bumped into Parson Weems. The men greeted one another affectionately, all anger forgotten.

"You must come and see Mrs. Carey," Mathew insisted.

He threw his arm over the shoulder of his old friend, and they walked along, as ill-assorted a pair as possibly could be seen on a street where an Indian might brush shoulders with a French count, or a slave meet a merchant. The parson had to break into a trot to keep up with the long uneven steps of his carefully dressed friend.

When the two appeared in the parlor doorway, Mrs. Carey dropped her sewing and greeted the little man warmly.

"Mr. Weems, you have been away too long," she said. "We've missed your ready wit. You must lodge with us while in town. I won't hear of any excuses."

In a very few minutes, talk turned to the books the Careys had stored on their shelves. Weems spoke up, saying that if only his employer would agree, he could find honest men to open branch stores throughout the South, and he, himself, would check on them at intervals.

For once Mathew was cautious. "Do you remember Mr. Mullin who decamped to Norfolk with my books?" he asked.

"I do," replied the parson, "and I admit he turned out to be a villain of the first water, but we caught him and returned the books. You lost not a penny by that transaction."

In an effort to overcome Mathew's reluctance, the parson insisted that any previous failure of his was due to inexperience.

Mathew shook his head. "When I think of how I broiled on the red-hot coals of torture on your account."

"Citizen Carey," the parson bristled, jumping to his feet, "I love you, I believe you honest, but I'll not be your slave. You can't say things like that!"

"Now, gentlemen," interposed Mrs. Carey, "you know you love one another, but I am afraid you love your arguments more. You need one another, so let's have done with contention. It is time we went to dinner."

Parson Weems once more became a Carey book agent and Mathew took over the publishing of *The Life of George Washington*. The relationship continued for twenty-five years. Mathew, frequently angered at the slipshod ways of his agent, often accused the parson of pushing his own book at the expense of other Carey books.

"But," argued the parson in reply, "you have a great deal of money lying in the bones of George, if you will but exert yourself to extract it. I am only trying to make a profit for you—and me."

It was well that someone was keeping the memory of the first president alive, for people were beginning to forget the ideals for which he had fought so bravely. Mathew often recalled the great leaders of the Revolution as he watched the greedy men of his day bicker and fight for power without any care for the good of the country.

He often thought of the great contrast between these small-minded men and his benefactor, the Marquis de Lafayette, who had been a true friend to America without hope of personal gain. Mathew Carey had kept in touch with the Marquis and followed his career in France since his return to that country in 1785. There, Lafayette had been shamefully treated because of his ideals, then had been captured and thrown into prison in Austria. Mathew, greatly distressed, sought some means of sending comfort. At last he found a way of shipping to the Marquis several hogsheads of his favorite tobacco.

In the meantime, Mathew was giving more time to banking. By 1806, when he was appointed a director of the Bank of the United States, he thoroughly understood the problems, and he was convinced that a strong central bank was necessary for keeping the country on a sound financial basis. It would steady the United States which was in a time of turmoil. Political parties were warring against one another instead of uniting to protest the hostile acts of foreign powers. The states had ratified the Constitution, but now found it difficult to give up their authority to a central government. Time and again some state threatened to secede.

In 1810, the charter of the Bank of the United States came up for renewal. Mathew's own party, the Democrats, was stubbornly opposed to the renewal of the charter, saying without cause, that it was the tool of the Bank of England. Mathew, in defiance of party, pressed for continuance of the central bank.

One night Carey attended a party meeting at Carpenter's Hall. The session was crowded and noisy. Mathew listened quietly until he heard a speaker shout, "Carey is a traitor to our party!"

Catcalls and applause followed. Mathew rose. When the noise had somewhat abated, he raised his voice and said:

"I, Mathew Carey, am a traitor neither to the Democrats nor, what is more important, to our country."

A silence fell over the hall and all eyes turned to the speaker.

"If you insist on putting party above country, I call the Democratic Party traitors," he continued.

Then he went on to say that as a citizen, he had the right to express his views.

John Binns, editor of the *Democratic Press*, rose to add his voice to Mathew's. "I disagree with your views, Mr. Carey," he said, "but so earnestly do I believe in free speech, that I will give you a hearing in the pages of my newspaper."

Mathew wrote sixteen essays on the subject of the bank, and Mr. Binns published them as he had promised. But Mathew Carey met opposition to his campaign on all sides. Even the directors, infected by partisan politics, refused to give him needed statistics to help his fight for renewal of the charter of their own bank.

"Why are you so bothered?" asked Bridget one evening as she sat beside her husband, busy at work on one of his pamphlets.

Mathew brushed the papers aside, rose and paced back and forth in agitation.

"I can't sit idly by and see us all ruined!" he stormed. Carey's voice rose and he shook his fist. "Do you willingly submit to being a pawn of politicians?"

Mrs. Carey playfully covered her ears with her hands. "Come sit down, dear," she urged. "You don't have to make a speech to me. I believe you, but what more can you do? You have already done more than your share."

Mathew drew up a chair beside the table, and glancing across at his wife, said mildly, "I do have a plan, my dear."

He ignored her smile and leaned forward to explain. He would go to Washington as an individual citizen to plead for renewal of the bank charter. Since he, a Democrat, would be going against his party, no one could accuse him of self-interest.

"The newspapers can ruin you, Mathew," protested Bridget.

Mathew could not be swayed. "I cannot let personal danger stand in my way," he said. "I shall stay only long enough to ensure winning, or know I have lost the cause."

The next morning, Mathew consulted with Henry as to the running of the business while he was away. His son, now seventeen, had done his work well in Baltimore, and since his return to Philadelphia, had been carrying on much of the trade by himself. In addition, he was acting as chief reader for the Carey publications, and in his spare time devouring every treatise on history and political economy he could lay his hands on.

"My absence means, Henry, that you will have to make final decisions," said his father. "Consult your mother. She is wise. I never do anything important unless I first discuss it with her."

After he had made all necessary arrangements, Mathew packed his bags and took the stage for Washington.

Each day for three months found Mathew in the visitors' gallery of the Senate. He listened carefully to the debates and each night wrote arguments for the bank and offered proof that the charges made against it were false. He explained that the Bank of the United States had no connection with the Bank of England; furthermore, it was an aid to state and city banks, not a hindrance to them. These essays he had printed at his own expense.

The second morning of his stay, he asked to go into the Senate chambers to place a copy of his pamphlet on each desk. The guard refused him permission to enter. Mathew went to the office of one of the Pennsylvania Senators, but was denied help.

"Then, I must do it the hard way," he told the Senator. "At least, I hope you will read this pamphlet before you attend the next session."

He handed the Senator a copy of his work, then left to call on each of the other members of Congress.

The carefully dressed man who limped from one office to another soon became a familiar figure to the Congressmen. He discussed the bank with them at every opportunity. Many found him convincing, for Mathew Carey argued with all his energy.

On February 20, 1811, the day the discussions ended and the poll was to be taken, Mathew sat alone in the visitors' gallery and kept tally as the ballots were cast. He knew he had failed to convince some Senators who insisted on voting with their party. Others needed no urging to vote favorably, but those in the uncommitted group gave Mathew concern.

Some Senators seemed undecided even as they were taking their seats on the Senate floor. The voting would be close, Carey knew, and, even at that late date, he could not forecast which way it would fall.

With three Senators not yet heard from, the vote stood seventeen for the charter, and fourteen against. For the first time, Mathew permitted himself to hope. He was sure he had convinced at least one of those three, but to his consternation, one after another rose to say "nay." The vote was tie, and the decision lay with Vice President George Clinton. After a few minutes of deliberation, the Vice President rose and cast his ballot against renewal of the charter.

Mathew picked up his hat and went to his hotel to pack his bags. Why, he asked himself, hadn't he discussed the matter more thoroughly with Mr. Clinton? He had never thought the vote would be tied, thus leaving the decision to one man. The bank would have to be liquidated, with all sorts of failures following in its wake.

Although he sensed impending trouble, Mathew Carey knew that he had done all one man could do for his country at the time.

10

THE OLIVE BRANCH

MATHEW CAREY returned home from Washington much depressed. But his spirits were soon to be restored by the news that his brother James had decided to seek his fortune in America. He wrote that he would shortly sail from Ireland on one of the ships owned by the Philadelphia importer and merchant Stephen Girard.

Mathew's face glowed as he read James's letter announcing his coming. Often over the years his mind had gone back to the home on Redmond's Hill and the loyal group that once surrounded him there. Often he had wondered if he would ever see any of his family again.

"But James doesn't give us the name of his ship!" he exclaimed to Bridget as he finished reading his brother's letter to her. Then he added quickly, "However, my friend Stephen Girard will know which of his vessels recently left Ireland."

Turning to Henry, he said, "Will you please go present my compliments to Mr. Girard and ask him when the ship is due to arrive."

Before long, Henry was back with the news that *The Good Friend* had called at the port of Dublin a few months before and was expected in Philadelphia any day. Mr. Girard would notify his father as soon as he himself received word.

Only a week later, a boy sent by Mr. Girard came to say that *The Good Friend* had been sighted on the Delaware River. There was much excitement in the Carey household. Henry ran to the stable to order the horse and carriage brought around. As soon as it drew up before the door, Mathew hurried out and trotted the horse down Chestnut Street toward the wharves. When he reached the dock, the ship was still a little offshore, but he could see James standing by the rail, peering down anxiously at the crowd gathering below.

"I would have recognized him anywhere," Mathew said to Stephen Girard who hurried up to stand beside him as they watched the passengers disembark.

The reunion of the Carey brothers was joyous. James brought messages from the whole family.

As they drove through the city, James's eyes roved over the busy scene: the many mercantile houses and banks; Christ Church where, Mathew told him, Dr. Franklin and General Washington had worshipped; the handsome private homes. Proudly Mathew drove around Carpenter's Hall where the first Continental Congress had met; then on to the square where stood Independence Hall, the site of the signing of the Declaration of Independence, and the courthouse where the Constitution of the United States had been framed. He pointed out to James the streets recently paved with round stones.

"Everything looks so new," James said. "I never saw streets so wide, and the trees are enormous."

"Within a two-mile walk you come to deep forest," Mathew told him, "yet here we have a flourishing city with all the luxuries of Europe."

"But those blanketed Indians we saw trading at the market stalls?" asked James. "Aren't they still savages?"

Mathew laughed. "You'll see many natives trading here," he replied. "They live peaceably nearby and make good citizens."

Before Mathew finished speaking, they had drawn up before the Carey home. Bridget, who had been watching, was at the door to welcome another Carey to America.

That evening they sat down to a hearty meal of fried chicken and new peas, topping it off with the ice cream for which Philadelphia was famous. After the meal, the children listened openmouthed to tales of Ireland and their relatives there. Then James told of his voyage and of the tense hours on shipboard after they had been sighted by a British man-of-war. It had given chase, but at the moment when the warship was gaining on them, a large clipper hove in view and they had been deserted for bigger game.

"If they had overhauled you, you would have been in England this moment," said Mathew, and explained that for some years Britain had been taking American seamen from ships and forcing them to serve in the British Navy. Not only were they impressing sailors, as this was called, but they claimed that any ship they boarded was theirs by right of seizure. These insults, plus the British attempt to forbid trade with France, were arousing Americans to the breaking point. Added to this, some thought that it was the British in Canada who had incited the Shawnee Indian Tecumseh and his brother the Prophet to attack the settlers on the Western frontier.

To Mathew, this pressure from England was a matter of great concern. He felt it his duty to write of the dangers facing the country, and in addition he talked of the matter whenever he could find an audience. Whenever he spoke of the matter at home, Mrs. Carey would ask if there were no better way than war.

"I'm afraid not," he said. "I detest violence, but there are times when men must employ it, or be branded as cowards."

At last the people were aroused to the fact that America

must fight to guard her economic as well as her political independence. The nation would no longer submit to England, who treated her as though she were still a colony.

War was declared on July 18, 1812, and Mathew was gratified that Henry, nearly nineteen, at once joined the Pennsylvania militia.

It was a peculiar war, for despite individual examples of bravery, especially on the part of the commanders of the tiny American Navy, many Americans worked against the cause. There was a difference in the zeal shown by the various states, and in general the campaigns were not well planned. Still the British, who were fighting against France at the same time, were not in a position to carry on a full-scale war either, and fought only halfheartedly.

As the war progressed, Mathew grew increasingly concerned at the selfishness of his fellow Americans who were constantly jockeying for power in complete disregard of the good of their country. Violent quarrels still raged between those demanding a strong centralized government and those who insisted on States' rights.

In an attempt to bring the country to its senses, Carey began a book that he called *The Olive Branch: a Plea for Peace.* He urged unity among the warring factions in the United States, appealing to the honor and patriotism of his readers to support the war effort and save the nation from ruin. At the same time he begged for home manufactures to provide employment and for the protection of agriculture. At times, as he was writing the book, he felt that he, a private citizen, was being presumptuous, but he knew that someone must write such a work, and no one else seemed inclined to do so.

The Olive Branch was published and drew criticism on all

sides. Yet it was so widely read that it went into a number of editions. After his book had appeared, Mathew found himself challenged wherever he went.

On a hot Fourth of July, he and his two sons strolled over to Independence Square to listen to the patriotic speeches. Henry wore his uniform and young Edward his Sunday best. The Square was decked in flags, and on a platform erected in front of the open doors of Independence Hall, prominent citizens sat with a guest speaker. Mathew had refused to join them, preferring to sit in the Square with his sons. The Careys found a shady spot and settled themselves as the speaker was presented.

More concerned about the heat than the speeches, many in the audience only half-listened until the man began a political tirade.

"The union of the states should be dissolved forthwith," he shouted. Then he went on to say that a citizen of Philadelphia was spreading falsehood about his fellow Americans. "Mathew Carey," he announced, "has written a book hypocritically called *The Olive Branch: a Plea for Peace*. The author of this book claims that some states are trying to prolong the war because of the profits they make from privateering. Others, Carey asserts, simply refuse to fight Great Britain."

As the speaker paused for breath, Mathew limped to the platform and asked to be heard. Stephen Girard, who was contributing enormous sums to the war effort, moved aside to give him room. Carey stood before the gathering and looked at the citizens, then solemnly said, "I, Mathew Carey, have not lied to you. Your leaders are bringing disaster to this country. Because I love America so dearly, I cannot stand idly by and see my country ruined." He then asked, "Do you want to live once more under the heel of Great Britain?"

A man from the rear of the crowd shouted, "We couldn't be worse off."

At this, cries of "Treason, treason," came from the audience.

Then Stephen Girard spoke from his place at Mathew's side, saying that although he had lost much shipping, he knew for certain that some merchants were becoming rich by privateering and were anxious for the war to continue.

"I tell you," shouted Carey, "until we stop squabbling among ourselves and realize we are no longer a few scattered colonies, we will never be a nation worthy to be classed with other powers! We should cease to count on importing everything we need and build up the manufactures of our own country."

Having made his point, Mathew turned and left the platform, followed by Stephen Girard. From all corners of the Square came applause and shouts for Carey.

Henry joined the two friends, but Edward had slipped away. Suddenly, from behind them came a sound of scuffling, and the men turned to see two boys on the ground pummeling one another. Henry stepped from his father's side and lifted Edward from the chest of his opponent.

"Let me at him," shouted Edward, struggling to free himself from his brother's grasp. "He called my father a crippled agitator."

"You can't object to that, son," Mathew said mildly. "Both statements are true. The first is not my fault, but the second is. All my life I've tried to stir people to action for their own good—and it is a thankless task."

A red-faced man who was dusting off the other little boy, turned and said, "Mr. Carey, my son was merely repeating a thoughtless remark of mine, for which I apologize. But I must say that you have me worried. My import business will be ruined by your insistence on home manufactures."

"On the contrary, sir," replied Mathew. "With many gainfully employed in industries at home, there will be more money to indulge in the luxuries you will import. Come, Edward. Good day, sir."

He bowed to the man, threw his arm around Edward's shoulder, and led his little group from the Square.

The second war with England dragged on. In 1813, the political officers in the American Army had been weeded out and professional soldiers put in command. The following year, important battles were won by the American forces, and although the British invaded Maryland and burned Washington, now the capital of the nation, they later withdrew as they were not strong enough to hold their position. The war ended in December, 1814, and a peace treaty was signed early the following year. Again, an ill-prepared militia had successfully defended the country against the forces of England, and American shipping was freed of the threat of attack and seizure on the seas.

During the next few years, American manufactures increased, and, to his satisfaction, Mathew saw that the immigrants who were pouring into the country were finding means of earning a living. Those who had come earlier were joined by their families. Just as James had followed him and had joined his brother's firm until he could start a business of his own, these new immigrants settled down quickly and worked to build up their adopted country. At last the United States gave promise of becoming a great nation. But it had a long way to go.

Mathew Carey was determined that the new-won freedom of the seas should not be used to flood the country with European goods. At every opportunity he urged the setting up of more home manufactures, no matter how small, and he preached patronage of these manufactures in his own home.

One evening, as the family was sitting together, Maria remarked, "Mrs. Elliott has opened a bonnet shop in her home on Third Street and has hired four women to sew for her."

Bridget looked up from her embroidery and said, "I always thought her own bonnets so pretty. Do you think she made them?"

"She'll never make a living," remarked Frances. "Who will buy from her now that Paris hats are becoming so plentiful and cheap?"

"Snobbery may ruin her," interrupted her father, looking up from his writing. Then, glancing around at his wife and daughters, he said, "But I know of at least five customers she will have. When I look at my millinery bills, I think she will not starve."

"But, Papa!" protested his daughters in chorus.

"Girls," said Bridget, "since your father pays your bills, and willingly, too, we will buy our hats at Mrs. Elliott's."

The girls were silenced, but Mathew continued to think about the problems of Mrs. Elliott and those like her. To guard them against foreign competition, they needed a protection that only their government could give them. A high tariff was needed to protect little businesses and help them expand so that more workers might be employed.

As a private citizen, Mathew determined to lend his support to this cause and began to gather material for a flood of pamphlets he was to write over the following years.

11

THE PATRIOT

CONCERNED as he was about the national welfare, Mathew Carey soon came upon another cause to defend. Now that Henry was married and the other children were grown, it was his pleasure to read to his wife each evening as she sat with her knitting. One day he stopped in the bookstore to select some interesting novels and came across Godwin's *Mandeville* that had just arrived from England. On glancing through it, Mathew saw the scene was laid in Ireland in the mid-seventeenth century. With a smile of anticipation, he tucked it under his arm and took it home.

That evening after he and Bridget were settled comfortably, he polished his glasses, then opened the book and began to read aloud. He had not read many pages before he slammed the book down and looked at his wife who had let her knitting fall in her lap as she gaped at him with a shocked expression on her face.

"What kind of novel is that, Mathew?" she demanded.

Mathew pounded the table in anger. "This vile book is the most popular novel in England today," he informed her. "Godwin is dragging up all the old lies about Ireland. He must be answered!"

Mathew went to his bookshelves and began to drag out volume after volume, muttering to himself all the while. For six months he read all the material he could find on the Irish insurrection of 1641. Then he wrote a book that he called *Vindiciae Hiberniae* in which he took the accusations against the Irish, and by comparing one author against another, painstakingly proved that the historians' assertions repeated by Godwin were wrong. The Irish had not planned an uprising, but had been goaded into one. Among other things, the number reported slain was larger than the whole population of Ireland at the time!

Mathew was proud of his defense of his native country and felt that his simple logic would convince even the British that the Irish had been libeled.

He planned to send his book abroad to prove his point, but the English authorities refused permission for it to enter the country. Through a friendly sea captain, Carey smuggled some copies to his brothers in Ireland, but, for the rest, had to be satisfied with the influence his book had on Americans.

Each passing year seemed to bring a new crisis in the expanding nation, and each was of personal concern to Mathew Carey. In 1820, a quarrel developed between the new bishop of Philadelphia and the lay trustees of the Catholic church of St. Mary's. It grew to such proportions that one Sunday in June of 1822, Maria returned from Mass and reported to Bridget and Mathew that St. Mary's Church was closed tight, and they had to go to Mass at St. Joseph's.

"The bishop preached," said Maria, "and said that the trustees had locked him out of the church."

Mathew looked across the breakfast table at his wife and shook his head, saying it was bad business to quarrel over religion.

He thought the new bishop should realize that problems in America were not the same as those in Europe. Here, with no priests in the community, laymen had formed associations and built churches, then invited the bishop to send a priest. Since the trustees were responsible before the law for conducting the association, they felt it their duty to have a say in the appointment of pastors, too.

The next day, Carey wrote a pamphlet advising concessions on both sides. No one heeded him, and the feud continued for several years. During that time, Mathew Carey came to realize that the bishop had right on his side and swung to his defense. At last the bishop's authority was recognized, and peace came to the diocese. The church disagreement seemed a part of the troubled times.

In 1824, the tariff issue was strongly to the fore and pamphlet after pamphlet was written, paid for, and circulated by Mathew Carey. Henry Clay, waging his campaign in Congress, read the pamphlets and thought Carey's reasoning clear. He wrote to the author and they entered into a lengthy correspondence. Some of Carey's letters to Henry Clay were later published under the title of *Prospects beyond the Rubicon*.

Once when Mathew went to Washington on business, he met the fiery Henry Clay. The Congressman invited him to

lunch and they chatted pleasantly while waiting for some of the other statesmen who were expected to join them.

"What do you stand to gain by a high tariff?" asked one man bluntly when the party was complete.

Carey half rose from his chair in wrath, then settled back saying, "A strong, independent country, sir!" Then he added, "That should be your aim and that of everyone here."

The man flushed, but before he could speak, another representative said, "The manufacturers themselves are not bringing much pressure to bear."

"Unfortunately, that is true," replied Mathew. "They don't seem to realize that unless we protect our small industries, they will be swallowed up."

On returning from his trip, Mathew said to his wife,

"Those men in Congress carry with them the huckstering habits of private life," and told her of the discussions with the men. Bridget listened sympathetically, then said Henry and his wife were coming to dinner. He might understand the problems involved better than she.

After dinner that night, Mathew told his son of his experiences in Washington, but curiously Henry was not in accord with his father's views.

"I'm not sure that I agree with you, Father, about high tariffs," he said. "I believe trade will increase if restrictions are removed."

"Can't you see, my boy," asked Mathew, "that free trade increases the miseries of the poor?"

He rose and paced the floor in agitation. Henry insisted that he could not understand his father's point.

"Now, Henry," said Mathew as he resumed his seat and leaned toward his son, "I know you think that if there is free trade the poor can buy at a lower price, but that means nothing if they cannot earn enough to buy at all. We must protect American industries so the manufacturer can afford to pay the workingman a fair salary."

"I had not looked at it that way," said Henry thoughtfully.

"You and I will manage if the country is flooded with foreign goods," continued Mathew. "But what is to happen to the widow and the poor immigrant who has agreed to repay the passage money lent him, but cannot earn enough to fulfill his debt? He has no alternative other than selling himself and his wife and children into bondage. Have you thought of them?"

"You have given alms to these people all your life," protested Henry.

"Charity is bitter, my boy. I wish there was no need for me to give another cent. If everyone had an opportunity to earn his own livelihood, our nation would be strong. In this country there is no need for poverty. All that is necessary is the remembering of the rights of our fellow man. I must write about that!"

So much time was Mathew devoting to his writings on these subjects that in the year 1822 he decided to retire from his now prosperous publishing business. Henry had been assuming more and more responsibility, and it seemed only fair to withdraw and turn the firm over to him. Besides, he would not have to bear the responsibility alone. Henry's sister Frances had married young Isaac Lea who had entered the Carey business soon afterward.

"There is only one request I have to make of you, Henry," Mathew said. "Be gentle with Parson Weems. He has grown old in our service."

Bridget, overhearing the request, laughed heartily. When Mathew's eyebrows shot up, she said, "Forgive me, my dear, but when have you ever been gentle with the parson? Kind and fair, yes, but gentle, no."

When the parson made his next call, Bridget could not resist telling him of Mathew's request to Henry. The parson joined in the laugh, then clapped his friend on the shoulder.

"You are gentle like a bull, my friend. Should Henry neglect your advice on that score, I wager I won't know the difference."

Then, choosing a chair near the fire, he leaned back, placed the tips of his fingers together and asked, "And what do you plan to do with your newfound leisure, may I ask?"

"I had every intention of devoting myself to home and

family," said Mathew sheepishly, "but—"

"What is the cause this time?" asked the parson. Mathew said that the Kentucky statesman and Congressman Henry Clay, with whose views Mathew had long agreed, was pressing for a protective tariff. Someone must back him.

"You should make a convincing pair," remarked the parson, "he with his oratory and you with your pen."

"All I intend to do is point out the needs of the people," retorted Mathew with some heat.

Parson Weems rose and said, 'You, my friend, are a patriot of the first clap, and I am proud of you, but I must now go to bed. I start early for home, and that old wagon jounces more each year."

Bridget hastened to light a candle, and Mathew rose to bid his friend good night. He stood with an arm around Bridget's shoulder as they watched him toil up the stairs.

Two years after retirement, in 1824, Mathew learned to his joy that Lafayette would be visiting America again. America, mindful of its debt to the brave man, had invited the Marquis to come to the United States to receive the homage of its grateful citizens. Lafayette accepted gladly, and from the moment he landed in New York was acclaimed as a friend and a hero. His admirers in Philadelphia eagerly awaited his arrival and made many plans for his reception. Mathew Carey was among the distinguished group of citizens selected to welcome the Marquis. They formed a procession led by the city troop and several brass bands. At the border of the city, Lafayette was greeted with a fanfare, then with the famous visitor in their midst, they paraded through the city. Cheering spectators lined the way and all

Philadelphia took on a festive air.

The next day, Mathew along with Henry and Edward, now a sturdy young man ready to go into the publishing business, called on Lafayette. After proudly presenting his sons, Mathew Carey said, "I have come, Monsieur le Marquis, to repay your loan of forty years ago."

"It was the best investment I ever made," said Lafayette, clasping Mathew's hand warmly. "I have followed your career, and you have repaid the loan many times in the good you have done."

"I'm still on the unpopular side, as you probably well know," said Mathew.

"And always will be, my friend," Lafayette returned. "Yet few have the courage to hold to their beliefs when they are under fire."

But now, Mathew told his friend, that was all past. He intended to spend his days away from strife, helping the orphaned and defenseless.

The Marquis smiled as he said, "But, my friend, is not the last what you have been doing all your life?"

Before Mathew could protest, other callers arrived, and the talk became general. Sadly, he took his leave of Lafayette, knowing they would not meet again.

On their way home, he and the boys stopped in the bookstore, for Parson Weems was expected there. Instead, he found the parson's son. "My father sent me in his place," he said to Mathew. "He caught fever on his last trip and hasn't been able to shake it off. I'm afraid he is very poorly, sir."

Mathew was much concerned. While Henry discussed business with the parson's son, he sent out for a favorite Carey remedy to send to his old friend. A few months after, word came from Beaufort that the parson had died. Mathew grieved at the loss of the little agent with whom he had fought so many verbal battles over the years.

Another, much deeper sorrow was to come to Mathew Carey. In October, 1829, his wife Bridget died. Mathew deeply mourned his wife. It seemed only yesterday that he had carried her across the threshold of their first simple home, and they had begun their lives together. Although his public life had been stormy, he could always count on Bridget to provide a calm haven to which he could return. He often thought of a remark made by Parson Weems:

"I wish, sir, you would confer calmly with the two best friends you have in this world: your conscience and Mrs. Carey." How true were those words.

After his wife's death, Mathew Carey continued to write on any subject that aroused his sympathies, be it slavery or the plight of the poor, particularly of working women. Always fiery in his statements, he never failed to arouse public discussion. He wrote and circulated so many more pamphlets on the tariff that he was blamed for the final passage of the bill.

In 1832, South Carolina published a nullification act in which this state declared it would no longer be bound by the high tariff on woolens and cottons. A tumultuous parade was held in the city of Columbia to celebrate the passage of this act. As a climax to the celebration, Henry Clay and Mathew Carey were burned in effigy.

When his daughter Maria read about the disgraceful affair, she burst into tears and cried, "Father, after all you've done for others! This is horrible!"

Mathew put his arm around her and assured her that it

would never happen again. He definitely was retiring from public life.

In 1838, Henry, following in his father's footsteps, turned the publishing business over to Isaac

Lea in order to devote the remainder of his life to study and research in social science. He still held to his belief in free trade, but Mathew could see that he was conceding to his views on many points. He now talked often of the duty of capital to labor. A few short years after his father's death, he was to come completely around to Mathew's way of thinking and to be known as America's foremost political economist.

In the meantime, Mathew held firmly to his vow to stay away from politics, yet he wrote constantly for one cause or another. Although neither he nor Henry had much formal schooling, Mathew believed in education. He urged the establishment of a college in Philadelphia that would stress such practical subjects as chemistry, botany, mineralogy, political economy, and modern language rather than the classical languages then taught. But his plan came to naught.

He had success, however, in helping to establish adult schools for immigrants. Shortly after he had come to America, he was distressed because so few of the immigrants could either read or write, and were thus deprived of any hope of improving themselves. Along with others, he had helped organize a school to teach these people on Sunday, the only time they were free. For almost forty years he had watched over these "Sunday Schools." Nothing delighted him more than to visit a class and to see men and women from all nations holding books in their workworn hands, spelling out their lessons.

He was embarrassed one day by a German woman who ran up and seized his hand, kissing it in the manner of the foreign countries. As he withdrew it hastily, she looked up and said in understandable English that thanks to him, she had learned to read and write.

"No longer do I go to those sweatshops," she said with emotion in her voice. "Now I work where I can breathe in God's clean air and I can keep my little girl with me."

During the depression of 1837, Mathew Carey, now old, feared his son Henry would go into bankruptcy, and offered to sell his own house and carriage to help him. Henry refused the offer, but cautioned his father to be careful of expenses. This advice was not heeded, for Mathew could not refuse the distressed families who came to him for aid.

Daily, as the weather permitted, he went for a carriage ride through his beloved city. To its citizens, the well-dressed old man was a familiar sight as he went about, on the alert to defend or chastise as seemed necessary to him.

On September 14, 1839, Mathew's horse shied on the cobbles, bolted and threw him from the carriage. He never recovered from the accident and died within a few days, his last moments attended by Father Moriarity, pastor of St. Augustine's Church, and the Reverend Dr. Gartland of the Church of St. John the Evangelist. He was buried in the churchyard of old St. Mary's.

Mathew Carey left many to mourn him. It was only after his death, when person after person came forward to express sympathy and gratitude, that the family realized the extent of his lifelong charities.

And over each of his eighty years, he had proved his courage in standing up for his beliefs and what he believed best for the good of the country he had adopted as his own. His love for America was nowhere better expressed than in the dedication he wrote for an edition of his best-known work, *The Olive Branch:*

"This book is dedicated to our country as a mark of gratitude for inestimable blessings enjoyed in liberty of person, liberty of property, and liberty of opinion, to a degree never exceeded in the world."

Author's Note

In Philadelphia, there is so much material on Mathew Carey that it was difficult to decide which to use for this book. In the Pennsylvania Historical Society library, I found diaries, letters, and even a passport giving a description of Mathew Carey. His *Autobiography* which appeared in the *New England Magazine* gave many details of his life. Bradsher's *Mathew Carey, Editor, Author and Publisher* (Columbia University, 1912) was of great help, as were the books and pamphlets that Carey wrote himself, especially *The Olive Branch*, 1815, and the *Brief Account of the Malignant Fever*, 1793.

The Independence Square neighborhood in which Carey lived for many years is being restored as a national shrine. I was able to see the area as he saw it over a hundred and fifty years ago.

For a picture of Ireland, I used many references, but the chief source of information was Creed's *All About Ireland*, Duell, 1951. Mr. Thomas P. Boden of Dublin checked on the streets and lanes Mathew walked as a boy. Mr. Boden rides through Redmond's Hill daily.

Mason Locke Weems must have saved every letter his

employer wrote him. They are included in a three-volume work entitled *Mason Locke Weems, His Work and Ways,* and were an invaluable aid in re-creating the relationship between the two men.

The *Sketch of the Life of Mathew Carey,* which Isaac Lea read before the American Philosophical Society on April 17, 1846, showed me the love the Carey family bore for Mathew. The *Letters* of Bridget Flahavan Carey emphasized her love for her husband.

My thanks are due to my fellow librarians and friends who lent me material and did courier service, but most of all I wish to acknowledge my debt to Mrs. Flora Strousse who read and reread my manuscript, offering much helpful advice.

www.ingramcontent.com/pod-product-compliance
Lightning Source LLC
LaVergne TN
LVHW051838080426
835512LV00018B/2952